G000115874

The God We Proclaim

The God We Proclaim

SERMONS ON THE APOSTLES' CREED

❧

edited by

John Hughes
and Andrew Davison

foreword by Graham Ward

with contributions by
John Hughes, Simon Oliver, Janet Soskice,
Matthew Bullimore, Simon Gathercole, Anna Williams,
Andrew Davison, Christopher Cocksworth,
Robert Mackley, and Sam Wells

CASCADE *Books* · Eugene, Oregon

THE GOD WE PROCLAIM
Sermons on the Apostles' Creed

Copyright © 2017 Wipf and Stock Publishers. All rights reserved. Except for brief quotations in critical publications or reviews, no part of this book may be reproduced in any manner without prior written permission from the publisher. Write: Permissions, Wipf and Stock Publishers, 199 W. 8th Ave., Suite 3, Eugene, OR 97401.

Cascade Books
An Imprint of Wipf and Stock Publishers
199 W. 8th Ave., Suite 3
Eugene, OR 97401

www.wipfandstock.com

PAPERBACK ISBN: 978-1-4982-9345-7
HARDCOVER ISBN: 978-1-4982-9347-1
EBOOK ISBN: 978-1-4982-9346-4

Cataloguing-in-Publication data:

Names: Hughes, John. | Davison, Andrew.

Title: The God we proclaim : sermons on the Apostles' Creed / Edited by John Hughes and Andrew Davison.

Description: Eugene, OR: Cascade Books, 2017 | Includes bibliographical references.

Identifiers: ISBN 978-1-4982-9345-7 (paperback) | ISBN 978-1-4982-9347-1 (hardcover) | ISBN 978-1-4982-9346-4 (ebook)

Subjects: LCSH: Apostles' Creed. | Apostles' Creed—Sermons. | Doctrinal preaching. | Title.

Classification: BT 993.3 .G58 2017 (print) | BT 993 (ebook)

Manufactured in the U.S.A.   DECEMBER 11, 2017

New Revised Standard Version Bible: Anglicized Edition, copyright 1989, 1995, Division of Christian Education of the National Council of the Churches of Christ in the United States of America. Used by permission. All rights reserved.

Also by John Hughes

The End of Work: Theological Critiques of Capitalism (Wiley-Blackwell, 2006)
The Unknown God: Sermons Responding to the New Atheism, editor (Cascade, 2013; SCM Press, 2013)
Graced Life: The Writings of John Hughes, edited by Matthew Bullimore (SCM Press, 2016)

Also by Andrew Davison

Amazing Love (DLT, 2016)
Blessing (Canterbury Press, 2014)
Care for the Dying: A Practical and Pastoral Guide, with Sioned Evans (Cascade, 2014; Canterbury Press, 2014)
Why Sacraments? (Cascade, 2013; SPCK, 2013)
The Love of Wisdom: An Introduction to Philosophy for Theologians (SCM Press, 2013)
Imaginative Apologetics: Theology, Philosophy and the Catholic Tradition, editor (SCM Press, 2011; Baker, 2012)
For the Parish: A Critique of Fresh Expressions, with Alison Milbank (SCM Press, 2010)
Lift Up Your Hearts, with Andrew Nunn and Toby Wright, editors (SPCK, 2010)

Table of Contents

Foreword: Believing

GRAHAM WARD

The gospel is simple, so anyone can understand it: repent, and believe in the Lord Jesus Christ who saved us from our sin and in whom we have life eternal. This is sufficient for faith, as countless numbers of Christians through the ages have found. It is accompanied by an injunction to pray and an exhortation (1 Tim 4:13) to read the Scriptures publically, preach and teach. Not all early Christians could read, especially because these "Scriptures" were in Greek (what is known as the Septuagint). Very few Jewish people, probably only the Pharisees who later became the rabbis, read them in Hebrew. So that is why others read them out publically, and offices or roles developed within the church so that the reading, preaching and teaching was available to all. There were no creeds. In fact, there was not even a standard and agreed upon set of Jewish Scriptures for the early church. The Christian New Testament took time to develop. Neither the rabbis nor the Christian church had finalized the canon of what we would consider to be the "Scriptures" today. But it was recognized that all Scripture is inspired by God and so useful for "teaching, rebuking, correcting and training in righteousness" (2 Tim 3:16).

Nevertheless, as the preaching and the teaching was faithfully carried out, questions arose that needed clarification; because people of faith are not stupid—they need to understand as far as possible what it is they are believing. The questions were different, depending upon what background the Christian came from. If they were Jewish there were questions about how Jesus, Lord

and Christ, was to be understood in the light of the Jewish traditions within which they had been brought up. If they were pagan
there were questions about the relationship of this historical man
with the divine, and what redemption actually meant. For both,
Jews and pagans, there was the question of "why now?"—why was
God acting now? And how was God's revelation of salvation now
related to all that had gone before and would follow after? And,
finally, there was the Holy Spirit in whom they were baptized. In
what relationship did the Holy Spirit stand to God as Father and
Jesus the Christ as Son?

So, from the beginning, there were questions and the creeds
as summaries of Christian teaching emerged from them. Slowly.
They have a curious history. What became known as the Apostles'
Creed and the official Nicene Creed took centuries to take shape.
The Old Roman Creed, the basis for the Apostles' Creed, only came
into existence halfway through the fourth century. The Apostles'
Creed as we have it today was not fixed until sometime around the
eighth century. The Council of Nicaea (325 CE) may have agreed
on a series of interlocking creedal formulae, but the creed wasn't
widely used and some bishops had never heard of it, so it had to
be reaffirmed with additions, at the First Council of Constantinople (381 CE). Then, because this was a highly disputed Council,
it was only following the Council of Chalcedon (451 CE) that the
Nicene Creed became truly catholic and ecumenical; catholic and
ecumenical, that is, only until the end of the eighth century when
the controversial *filioque* clause was inserted.

The curious histories of two of most the widely used creeds
today is important because it means that early Christians *believed*
when there was no definitive set of statements prescribing *what*
they believed. There were a lot of questions. As the preaching,
the teaching and the baptizing continued, and as these teachers
and preachers read and formed the canon of what became the
Scriptures, a greater collective understand of the Christian faith
emerged. Brief summaries of the Christian "gospel" are found in
the letters of Paul and early Christian texts like the *Didache*, and
early "rules of faith" were used to instruct those being baptized.

But the grand architectural form of the creeds was something un-available for three centuries.

So how did these early Christians achieve any sense of a shared identity without the support of creedal formulations and a closed scriptural canon that made a judgement about what God did and what God did not inspire? The Letters to Timothy actu-ally help us to see: the emphasis was on actions—public reading, preaching, teaching, and training in righteousness. And what was acted and enacted was a singular story eventually honed into the four distinct Gospels (attested to by the apostles), a series of letters crisscrossing the Mediterranean, and the Hebrew Bible (though translated into Greek). The Christian faith was practiced and Christian doctrine was lived in and through these stories—their telling, reading, preaching, and retelling—and the questions they provoked.

It is out of the accumulative experiences of those practices and that living that the creeds issued. They are not stand-alone confessions of what a Christian community accepts as truth over against the doctrinal claims of other Christian communities—as the Reformation confessions and articles of the faith were. They do not have the binding force of those agreements in their miniscule typefaces that we continually have to accept in order to update our computer software. They are not loyalty cards. They are ex-pressions, evolved over centuries, of what the church had come to understand about the faith it had been practicing and living as it preached and taught and trained. Whatever the politics at Ni-caea—and every dignitary present was waist-high in complex cur-rents and undercurrents—the agreement reached at the Council there in 325 CE and ratified, albeit in a slightly expanded form, at the Council of Constantinople, was a vast act of ecclesial discern-ment. The Nicene Creed was the distillation of catholicity from all that had been learnt through numerous readings of the Scriptures they had and were forming, liturgies, sacramental rites, prayers, preaching, errors and the correction of errors from the very ori-gins of the church in Jerusalem. It expressed lived doctrine and ac-cumulated Christian experience. It was intended not as some great wall protecting orthodoxy, but a framework for the continuation of what the church had always committed itself to doing: reading, preaching, teaching, and training the story in which their lives were now inserted.

One of the first public uses of a Creed that we have evidence of comes from Cyril of Jerusalem and his *Catechetical Lectures* for Lent 348 CE. The bishop delivered these lectures in the monumental and newly constructed basilica in Jerusalem that housed the sites of both the crucifixion at Golgotha and the resurrection tomb. The creed that those seeking baptism on Easter Eve were taught was not exactly the Nicene Creed—there were so many different creeds around at the time—but it is close. But most importantly, in being taught they were *not* given the creed in the early sessions, and when they were finally given it they were firmly told not to write it down. The creed had to be memorized; each discrete formula was to be internalized. All good teaching is a training that is to be internalized if it is to inform behaviours, attitudes, affections, and dispositions that are deeper than cognition and reasoning.

One of the major developments of the last thirty years has been in the recognition that our thinking is profoundly embodied and that we grasp only a small percentage of what is going on inside us. Most of the memorizing that goes with practices, for example, is laid down in sleep! Neuroscientists talk about perhaps 5 percent of what we experience as consciously available to us. Because of this *believing* has taken on new dimensions and depths. It is no longer understood as just a weak form of knowledge or opinion on some scale of probability and improbability. Believing taps into emotions and memories that are unconscious, subconscious, and preconscious. We believe far more than we know, acting upon those beliefs continually as we negotiate our experiences of the world. This is significant because Christian believing is not then some anti-rational surrender of intelligence or a leap in the dark; it is an orientation of a very human and very ordinary operation whereby we think through and grope our way towards an understanding of what it is to be alive and conscious. Our beliefs—their form, adaptation, modification, and morphing—have existential weight: for our happiness, sadness, senses of well-being or lack of it depend upon them.

The existential foundation of the Christian faith is an act of entrustment to Christ and this is rooted in longings and hungers that cognition and rationalization can only skim the surfaces of. And if we ask "Who is this Christ?", well, the same question can be heard throughout the Gospels whenever people encountered Jesus Christ in his teaching and working of miracles. The Gospels and the creeds give us a handful of titles—"Son", "Messiah", "Lord"— but these do not get at the relation that is established and the learning that has to take place through our entrustment to Christ. The answer to the question "Who?", like the doctrines of the Christian faith as a whole, has to emerge from the ongoing enactment of that trust, the ongoing framing of one's experience by that trust. Given this, and what I have said about the nature of believing (whether religious or non-religious), Christian believing is not about an isolated act of will. There may be a moment of decision, but all the inner and outer operations of self and world that have brought us to that decision are given expression *in* that decision *as* that decision. Christian believing is not an act of fully comprehending all that Christian doctrine apprehends. It is a stretching, as every animal and human movement is a step towards something: a loss and an acquisition. It is a reaching back into oneself as much as a reaching out into the world; for all things, we are repeatedly told by Paul, are *in* Christ.

In Acts Paul is recorded as giving a magnificent address before the Areopagus. In that address, he reminds the Greek intellectuals assembled in their capital city of an altar that have erected "To an Unknown God". On the basis of this altar, he then proclaims the God who is the Creator of all things and who, in that creation, ordained that human beings should be part of it: "They were to seek God, and, it might be, touch and find him; though indeed he is not far from each one of us, for in him we live and move, in him we exist" (Acts 17:27). The Greek for "touch and find him" describes the act of our groping forwards in our daily encounters with the invisible in the visible. The attempt to grasp each of the articles of the Christian faith, formulated in the creeds, and the way the articles of the Christian faith relate coherently to each other, is a groping towards that divine knowledge of truth in Christ and towards understanding the purpose of our creation. As such the Creeds are, again, lived as the tradition is lived, and so we can say, as Augustine once said, "We believe that we might understand."

Graham Ward

Introduction: John Mark Hughes (1978–2014)

ANDREW DAVISON

John Hughes was a terrific preacher. His death in June 2014, at the age of thirty-five, has deprived us of one of the leading British Christian thinkers of his generation. A theologian, philosopher, ethicist, and pastor, John was also one of the most vivacious and joyful human beings those of us who knew him are ever likely to encounter.

Everything he did sprang from his vocation as a priest, and little was more central to his sense of priesthood than the work of preaching. The larger part of his sermons were written as week-by-week homilies at the Sunday morning Eucharist, most recently as chaplain, then dean, of Jesus College, Cambridge. On a Sunday evening, however, the sermons at college evensong were only sometimes delivered by him, and more often by a visiting preacher. That might have been a disappointing substitution, given John's abilities as a preacher, were it not for the breadth and calibre of the preachers he could call upon to fill the Sunday evening roster.

This collection, *The God We Proclaim: Sermons on the Apostles' Creed*, offers a snapshot of the preaching in Jesus College chapel over a single term: Lent Term 2013.[1] As is the tradition in Cambridge chapels—far more that at Oxford, where John also

---

1. A previous volume published by Cascade and SCM Press collects the sermons from an earlier term: *The Unknown God: Sermons Responding to the New Atheism* (2013).

studied—these sermons form an integrated series: as the subtitle suggests, an exposition of the Apostles' Creed. In bringing this collection to publication, I hope that it will contribute to the ongoing task to which John was so cheerfully devoted, the task of teaching the Christian faith, clearly and with enthusiasm.

A collection of John's academic writing has been published by SCM Press in 2016 as *Graced Life: The Writings of John Hughes (1979–2014)*, edited by Matthew Bullimore. I am grateful to Dr Elizabeth Powell for her work on the manuscript of this collection.

List of Contributors

The Revd Dr Matthew Bullimore, Vicar of St John the Baptist, Royston, and Priest in Charge of St Peter, Felkirk, and now vice-principal of Westcott House, Cambridge

The Rt Revd Dr Christopher Cocksworth, Bishop of Coventry

The Dr Andrew Davison, Tutor in Doctrine at Westcott House, Cambridge, and now Starbridge Lecturer in Theology and Natural Science, University of Cambridge, Fellow of Corpus Christi College, Cambridge, and Canon Philosopher of St Albans Cathedral

Dr Simon Gathercole, Reader in New Testament Studies, University of Cambridge, and Fellow of Fitzwilliam College, Cambridge

The Revd Dr John Hughes, Dean and Fellow, Jesus College, Cambridge, until his death in 2014

The Revd Dr Robert Mackley, Vicar of St Mary the Less, Cambridge

The Revd Canon Professor Simon Oliver, Professor of Christian Theology, University of Nottingham, and now Van Mildert Professor of Divinity, University of Durham

Professor Janet Soskice, Professor of Philosophical Theology, University of Cambridge, and Fellow of Jesus College

The Revd Canon Professor Graham Ward, Regius Professor of Divinity at the University of Oxford, and Fellow of Christchurch, Oxford

The Revd Dr Sam Wells, Vicar of St Martin-in-the-Fields, London

Dr Anna Williams, theologian and author

1

"I believe..."

JOHN HUGHES

Genesis 12:1–9
Mark 9:14–28

"Lord, I believe; help my unbelief!" (Mark 9:24)

Some of you may have seen the news reports of the 2011 United Kingdom census: that the proportion of people describing themselves as Christian in Britain has declined by 13 percent in ten years: from 72 percent to 59 percent. This is undoubtedly a disturbing statistic Christians in Britain, although we should probably take the advice of the former Archbishop of Canterbury and new Master of Magdalene, Rowan Williams, in his Christmas sermon. He reminded us that the picture is more complex than we think, and that in the end our faith is not based upon success or popularity but upon truth.

I've spoken in chapel before about so-called "cultural Christianity", which is what I think this statistic is mainly about, but tonight I want to spend some time reflecting on another issue which came up in the debate about the census results: what does *belief* mean? Any attempt to measure belief comes across this problem:

you can ask people what they believe, but sometimes their answers don't quite seem to add up, or else other evidence makes you wonder whether this is really so. Hence, we've seen the National Secular Society and others insisting that most of those who call themselves Christians are not really, because they don't really believe what they're supposed to, and so on. Sociologists have even spoken of contemporary religion in the West as being about "belonging without believing". In the light of all this, it seems worth beginning our series of sermons on the Apostles' Creed this term by pausing to think about the verb at the very beginning of that ancient universal statement of Christian belief. What does it mean to say "I believe . . ."?

In brief, I want to suggest that most of the ways we think about belief are unhelpful and inaccurate, and should be turned on their head. If we listen to how the language of belief is used in contemporary culture, leaving aside the narrowly "religious" uses, we find that belief is associated with one side of a set of polar oppositions. From pop songs to politicians' speeches, it is presumed that belief is something uncertain, irrational, private, and inside us (whether in the mind or the will or the feelings). So we say we "believe that something is the case" when we think it is probable that it might be so, but we're not sure, or when we have a private taste about something. This highly individualist way of thinking about belief has been very influential for the last few hundred years in the West, and it all too easily places belief—at best—in the realm of something to be practised in private between consenting adults, or at worst something childish to be overcome by adults. This was brought home to me when I once asked a child if he believed in God and he replied yes, before moving on quite naturally to talk about whether he believed in Father Christmas and the tooth fairy.

Against this way of thinking, I want to suggest, following a certain philosopher buried not so far from here (Ludwig Wittgenstein), that belief is not so much something that we do with our heads, or even with our hearts alone, but just as much with our *bodies*, and that, because of this, belief is not just something private or personal, but very much collective, corporate, and public.

In some ways, this is a very Anglican approach to belief, following on from Queen Elizabeth I's famous line about the impossibility of making windows into people's souls. It also has a certain psychological plausibility, for which of us can really say that we completely know even ourselves? But I would argue it is also much more biblical. The word for belief in Hebrew is related to Amen, and to the words for truth and trust. When we hear that "Abraham believed God" (Rom 4:3) it does not mean that Abraham had a special opinion about God, or a funny feeling about him: it means he entered into a relationship of trust that shaped the course of his life. Belief is first of all this personal relationship of trust, concerning the whole person. Abraham believing in God is not just about something inside him; it's about a relationship that makes him get up from Ur and go somewhere new. "By their fruits you will know them", says Christ (Matt 7:16). If you want to know what people believe, then it's better to look at what they *do* rather than what they *say*, or even *think*. Belief is about the shape of an entire life.

But what about certainty? Belief does seem to have something to do with uncertainty, or else why would everyone not just agree about it? One of the most famous verses of Scripture on belief could seem to support this view by contrasting belief with the certainty of sight. This is when the Letter to the Hebrews speaks of faith as "the substance of things hoped for, the assurance of things not seen" (11:1). But surely the contrast here is more like the difference between being on a journey and the end of that journey. The uncertainty of belief is more to do with the fundamental glorious openness of life itself, since the nature of life is such that we can respond to it in different ways, and the differences between these ways are not something that could ever be finally resolved in this life. This is precisely why a proper understanding of belief should support the freedom of people to hold differing beliefs rather than trying to coerce everyone to believe the same thing. Christ *calls* people to follow him *because* we have the freedom to do so.

But this openness is not quite the same as saying that belief is something optional, a niche interest for those who are into that kind of thing, like jogging or vegetarianism: for if belief is about what you do with your body, the shape of a life, then simply to live is to believe something, whether we realise it or not. Our lives are always already oriented towards certain views of the world, implicitly presuming certain things to be of value or not, whether we chose these directions or not. The question then is not whether you will believe or not, but rather in what, and whether you will realise or not! And when we think of belief in terms of the underlying commitments that shape a life, we realise that, while in one way belief may be characterised by less certainty than my knowledge of dull facts, such as the existence of a table in my study, in other ways belief concerns the things held to with *most* certainty. Most facts are generally rather uninteresting things to die for, but not beliefs!

All this does not mean that belief is something irrational. It may be beyond straightforward logical demonstration, it may be a matter of the whole person rather than something narrowly intellectual, but belief should not be the end of intellectual curiosity, criticism and thinking. Much more could be said about all this, but suffice it to say that being a theologian would be very dull if it were not so! The reason we have theology in universities is because belief is not the end of questioning and understanding, but rather its beginning. And I think this is true not just for theologians, but for most Christians, who don't want to leave their brains at the doors of the church. The relationship with God that we call belief is, like any relationship, a constant journey of understanding. I rather like the picture of Jacob wrestling with the angel from our Old Testament reading as a symbol for this side of faith. The psalms and the book of Job are other great places to look for examples of belief as a pretty robust and honest relationship.

But all this can sound rather exhausting, as if belief is a rather dysfunctional relationship, all about hips getting put out of joint (as happened to Jacob). Perhaps the most surprising and important thing about belief is when we discover that it is not in the end all about us at all. We might contrast the comment that people sometimes make about their faith "coming and going". I think this must be what they mean: that faith is like a feeling, which sometimes they get and sometimes they don't, or that it's like an act of will which sometimes they can manage and sometimes they can't. This is the real core to the modern individualistic view of belief. "I believe" becomes here some great act of self-projection, an extension of our will. And yet belief in the Scriptures is much more like a gift, something we simply receive. I think this is usually true of most relationships—however hard we work at them, we can't *make* someone love us. Indeed friendship and love is usually something like a gift that releases us from these rather pathetic strivings. The theological word for this is "grace".

Mercifully, we do not all have to sit down and make up our own creed from scratch. The Creed is given to us, like the church itself, because we do not believe on our own. Belief *is* bound up with belonging, because it is something like inhabiting a landscape, exploring a vision, and we do this in the company of others. Ultimately, however, belief is not just something we receive from other humans, from the church. If belief is a relationship with God, then that relationship is a gift which he offers us, rather like the outstretched hand Christ offered to the sinking Peter on the Sea of Galilee. The prayer of the father of the child in our New Testament reading tonight captures this paradox well: "Lord I believe, help my unbelief!" We start off by thinking belief is all about us, something we do, and then discover that it is a gift to be received, something for which to pray. Some days we may feel like a mighty warrior of faith; other days we may feel we have less faith than a mustard seed. Some days we may think we understand it all; others we may feel completely mystified. But it does not matter. The Christian faith, which the Apostles' Creed summarises, is not all about us. It is about the God who created all things and who invites us to explore the infinite riches of the relationship that he offers us in Jesus Christ. To him be glory and praise, now and forever, Amen.

2

"In God the Father Almighty, Maker of heaven and earth"

SIMON OLIVER

Exodus 3:1–15
John 1:1–14

In 1692, an ambitious clergyman, Richard Bentley, later a controversial Master of Trinity College (he endured a thirty-year feud with the College's Fellows), was commissioned to deliver the first Boyle Lecture. Robert Boyle, the great natural philosopher, had died the previous year. He endowed a series of lectures for the discussion amongst learned men of the existence of God. In preparing his lecture, Bentley wrote to the Lucasian Professor, Isaac Newton, to ask about the usefulness of his great work, *Principia Mathematica*, for the defence of the faith. In a now oft-quoted letter, Newton replied, "When I wrote my treatise about our Systeme [the *Principia*] I had an eye upon such Principles as might work with considering men for the belief of a Deity and nothing can rejoice me more than to find it useful for that purpose." In the same letter, Newton states that he was forced to ascribe the design of the solar system to a voluntary agent and, moreover, "the motions which the Planets now have could not spring from any natural cause alone but were impressed by an intelligent agent."

While Newton wrote far more about theology and prophecy than he did about natural philosophy, it is his physics that transformed our perception of the universe. Nevertheless, Newton was part of a wider pattern that emerged during the eighteenth and nineteenth centuries, in which a particular way of understanding creation and divine providence became dominant: the view that God had designed the universe. This reached its most influential expression in William Paley's *Natural Theology*, published in 1802. It's often thought that the view that creation is designed is dominant throughout the Christian, and indeed philosophical, tradition, extending all the way back to Plato's *Timaeus* written in the fourth century BC. It's striking that New Atheists' attacks on religion tend to assume that, if we are to talk of God's act of creation, we must think in terms of God designing the universe in much the same way as I might design a car. Newton pictures creation in just this way: the matter of the universe is essentially passive and God decrees the laws of nature in the language of mathematics and then ensures that every element of the universe obeys the laws. Much as a monarch might govern a kingdom via the force of his legal decrees, so God governs the universe. This is apparently how we are to understand the first line of the Creed. To profess that God created heaven and earth is to say that God designs the universe: there is a direct similarity between the intentional human design of an artefact and God's "intelligent design" of the cosmos.

In fact, prior to this "theological revolution" of the seventeenth century onwards, the Jewish, Christian, and Islamic traditions do not understand divine creation in this way. There is a very striking consensus amongst religious thinkers over fifteen hundred years that if we are to speak of God's act of creation at all, we must speak of God's creating out of nothing. This is a baffling teaching. What's it about?

First, the tradition is clear that whatever we mean by creation, we cannot be talking about a natural process. In other words, we are not talking about one thing coming from another. Why? Because any natural process belongs *within* creation; it cannot be the source *of* creation. To stop us talking about God's creative act as if it were just another event, ancient and medieval theologians, and many philosophers, deemed it better to talk of the utterly unique and originate act of creation as, paradoxically, "from nothing". Secondly, creation out of nothing doesn't look back exclusively to an original moment, a kind of "Big Bang" billions of years ago, and say "that first and original moment is the most important; crack that, and you've understood the universe." Instead, creation out of nothing suggests that *at every moment* the universe is created and sustained by God. This moment now is just as new, just as revealing, as the first moment of creation, whenever that might have been. For the Jewish tradition in particular, to express the view that God continually sustains creation in existence is part-and-parcel of the profession that God is continually present in history and eternity as existence itself, the great "I AM" (Exod 3:14), the name of God given to Moses about which we heard in our first reading.

So creation out of nothing is an attempt to stop us talking about God's act of creation as if it were a bigger and grander version of human beings making things. God does not take some pre-existent stuff and impose an order on it from outside. When God creates, there is not one thing—God—and then suddenly two things—God plus creation standing alongside. There is one source of existence, the "I AM", and all creation is, at every moment, sharing in that eternal source. This ancient way of understanding God's creative act is not explanatory in anything like the scientific sense. It is a check on idolatry, on thinking that God is a human being writ large.

In fact, creation out of nothing is not so much an attempt to say something about creation as it is to say something about God. If we are to talk of God at all, we talk of the divine's complete and sovereign freedom. When I make something, I am in some sense constrained by the materials I work with, or by my own limitations. God is not so constrained by some pre-existent stuff which challenges God. God is not a manufacturer of the cosmos but is, as the Creed puts it, the *Creatorem caeli et terrae*, the *Creator* of heaven and earth. There is no compulsion or necessity to creation, but it is an expression of God's eternal self.

It seems to me that this leads us to what is perhaps the most important aspect of the profession that God is Creator, and Creator out of nothing: creation is a gift. For the Abrahamic traditions, the universe is not a brute fact nor the inexplicable outcome of a blind process. It is a gift, which is the expression of love, the free and completely unnecessary donation of existence and life. This is, if you like, "the Christian difference" that emerges from our profession of God as Creator: the difference that comes from living one's life not as a right or a chance happening in the corner of a dark and cold universe, but as a gift. Why does this make a difference? We know that gifts express a relationship. When my sons make something at school, which they bring home as a gift for their parents, that gift expresses something of who they are and their relationship to us, their parents. The gift mediates that relationship. Similarly, our lives are understood as an expression of a relationship with the source and giver of life. Secondly, a gift in some sense places an obligation on the recipient and invites a response. There is a particular way to treat a gift that is different from the way we treat other things; we treasure it, value it, enjoy it, nurture it, and make good use of it as an expression of the love of the donor. And to understand life as a gift provokes a particular and primary response from us; it provokes gratitude. This is why the New Testament is littered with a simple injunction: be thankful. Here's the Letter to the Colossians: "And let the peace of Christ rule in your hearts, to which indeed you were called in the one body. And be thankful . . . . And whatever you do, in word or deed, do everything in the name of the Lord Jesus, giving thanks to God the Father through him" (Col 3:15). To live in a way that Christians have described as "eucharistic", as thankful, is an outworking of our profession that God is *Creatorem caeli et terrae*, the source of all being and life. Surely to understand creation as a gift rather than a brute fact, which we turn into a natural resource for economic exploitation, would result in a very different attitude to the natural world.

For too long the Christian doctrine of creation has been thought to be a competitor to scientific cosmology. The Newtonian view of a designer God who ruled the universe from a distance was to have very serious consequences for our understanding of what it means to profess "creation". In the end, such a God was rightly deemed dispensable in the face of the advances of the natural sciences. However, for the Christian tradition, as the opening of Saint John's gospel puts it, all things were created through God's Word or reason. Creation expresses this eternal reason and order, which is not imposed from without onto pre-existent material. Creation is intrinsically an expression of God's Word, God's eternal reason. So we can make sense of nature's processes through *our* use of reason in the natural sciences. But God's Word is also given again in the incarnation for our salvation. Creation is revealed as God's utterly free and gratuitous gift of existence and life, which is given again and again in Jesus Christ, even when that gift is abused and refused. It is given again that, professing that God is Creator of heaven and earth, we might live truly thankful lives in God's love and treasure that gift as a sign of love.

3

"And in Jesus Christ his only Son our Lord"

JANET SOSKICE

Hosea 6:1–3
Philippians 2:5–11

Possibly the worst way to introduce someone to the Christian faith is to give them a copy of the Apostles' Creed. Give them a Bible instead or better, read one with them. This is not because Christians don't "believe" that to which the Creed attests or because the Creed is not biblical, for certainly it is, but because the Creeds were never intended to be explanatory. They are a means by which one confesses the faith, not a means to explicate it. In the early church a postulant would study Scripture and Christian teaching for many weeks and even months before, usually at Easter time, being presented for baptism and publicly confessing the Creed. The Creed would not be an explanation but a telegraphic summary of all they had imbibed during their period of instruction. Many of us, here I speak from experience, have come at it the other way. We have heard the Creed, recited the Creed, even confessed the Creed many times without much teaching as to what it might mean, and in these circumstances the Creed can be frankly baffling.

Let's begin then with the idea that the Creeds are condensed expressions of faith and praise in the One we confess to be our

Maker and Redeemer.[1] I say "the One" who is our Maker and Redeemer because the Creeds are a confession of belief in One God: Father, Son, and Holy Spirit. These are not three gods, nor even three bits of the one God but One God who is our Maker and Redeemer. It was by way of underscoring this that medieval theologians sometimes spoke of the Creeds as the Christian equivalent of the Jewish *Shema*—the central Jewish prayer drawn from the Book of Deuteronomy: "Hear, O Israel: the Lord our God, the Lord is One" (Deut 6:4). The contention that the Apostles' Creed is a Christian variant on the *Shema* seems odd at first, but the followers of Jesus insisted from the outset that theirs was a monotheistic faith, worshipping one God, and the Creeds are its condensed expression.[2] In older books of worship the Creed is presented as just one sentence, admittedly a lengthy one. Here I have to hand it to Wikipedia, who in their online version (at least at time of writing) present the Apostles' Creed as just one sentence divided into twelve sections by colons. Grammar underscores content—we are confessing belief in One God.

After the initial declaration that "I believe in God the Father, Almighty, Maker of heaven and earth", the following six verses, constituting nearly half of the whole, concern Jesus: his conception and birth, his crucifixion, his death, burial and resurrection, not to mention his descent into hell, and anticipated return to judge the living and the dead. I will not even attempt the finer points of all these extraordinary claims. What I will address is a crucial question, the one on which all the others depend. It is this: "Who is this

1. They are many other things, of course. A church historian would say that they are formularies settled upon to resolve contentious disputes in the early church. On these, and for a good general introduction, see Wilken, *The First Thousand Years.*

2. There were individuals and movements who held out, for instance for a something like a bitheism where Jesus and his Father were two gods, but the dominant understanding was monotheistic, and this seems attested in the New Testament writings themselves. On the debates see James Dunn, *Did the First Christians Worship Jesus?*, and Larry Hurtado, *How on Earth Did Jesus become a God?* Very illuminating on this, if you want a biblical commentary on that most Jewish of all books of the New Testament, is Richard Bauckham, *The Theology of the Book of Revelation.*

Jesus? Who is this one who was crucified, dead and buried, who was raised and in whom our hope of redemption resides?" By way of reply I'll look at "I believe in Jesus Christ, his only begotten Son, our LORD", and my focus will be on the names of God.

In the first line of the Creed we have been give three divine titles or names—the *Father*, the *Almighty*, and the *Maker* of Heaven and Earth. In the verse under consideration here we have three more: "And in Jesus *Christ*, his *only begotten Son*, our LORD". Christ, Son and Lord: it is this Jesus who we will then go on to confess to have been "conceived by the Holy Ghost and born of the Virgin Mary". Let's look at them more closely. "Son" and "Lord", as titles anyway, are quite familiar to us—we all know many people (technically all male people) who are somebody's "son", and in Britain we even have a smattering of "Lords"; "Christs" are more rare but the title means simply, in Greek, *the Anointed One*. Here in the Apostles' Creed, which was originally written in Greek, it is doing the same service as "Messiah" in the Old Testament, "Messiah" being the Hebrew for "the Anointed One".

Which of these three names or titles is the most exalted? We might think it would be calling Jesus "the Christ"—Jesus Christ, only Son and Lord. However I wish to suggest this is not the case. To claim someone is the "Anointed One" is not necessarily to claim this person is a God, or even a prophet. Many Jews at the time of Jesus looked forward to a Messiah or redeemer but in the expectation this would be a favoured person, maybe even a good King.

We get a bolder claim when we move beyond "Christ" to the second title "Son". We are by now all so familiar with, not to say jaded by, the Enlightenment rhetoric of the fatherhood of God and the brotherhood of man that we fail to notice that God, in the Old Testament, was almost never referred to as "father", and never addressed as "father" in prayer. It is striking then, that in the Gospels Jesus almost never addresses God with any other title that of "father".[3] In two dramatic New Testament instances, God names Jesus as his Son—at the time of the baptism of Jesus by John (Matt 3:17; Mark 1:11), and on the mountain when, in prayer, Jesus is

---

3. See Soskice, "Calling God 'Father,'" 66–83.

transfigured before his disciples who hear a voice from heaven saying, "this is my Beloved Son" (Matt 17:5; Luke 9:35).

My husband, not a theologian, surprised me not so long ago by saying "I know why Jesus is called the "Son of God" but I don't like it very much!" What, I thought, does he mean? He explained: Joseph is not the biological father of Jesus and Mary is a virgin, etc., etc. Now, however exalted a view we may have of the virgin birth this is almost certainly not what the Creed intends in naming Jesus as the Son. Think instead of the Scriptures. For the first Christians, most of them Jews or Gentile camp-followers familiar with Jewish Scriptures, a heavenly voice declaring that "this is my beloved Son" would immediately recall other "beloved sons"—not necessarily oldest sons, but sons on whom the promise of God rests. We must think of Joseph, of Jacob, and above all of Isaac, the son of Abraham, who had been asked to take his son, "your beloved Son", to the mountain and to sacrifice him (Gen 22). God, in the event, intervenes and supplies a ram that is sacrificed instead of the boy, and Isaac, the beloved Son, goes on to be the father of the people Israel. All these were sons of human fathers, but the "son of promise" named Jesus is, the Creed confesses, the Son of God.

The Nicene Creed underscores the importance by naming Jesus not only as "Son" but as "only begotten Son"—the distinction is between what is begotten and what is made. We creatures are made: bumble bees are made, daffodils are made, gravity is made—all these things are creatures. But Jesus is the Son begotten of the Father, one with his very being. That Creed goes on: "God from God, light from light, True God from True God, begotten not made, being of one Substance with the Father, through who all things were made". Here that Creed echoes the Gospel of John, where Jesus is identified (in chapter 1) with the Word who is eternally with the Father, through whom all things were made. So to say Jesus is the "only begotten Son", the "begotten", and therefore the "uncreated" Son of the Father, is no small claim. It is to put this son of promise on the divine side of the foundational distinction between God and "all that is", that is, creation.

Having considered what it might mean to say that Jesus is the "Christ" and the "Son" and turn finally to *our Lord*. This seems at the outset fairly easy to understand as a title. To call someone "Lord," except in the ceremonial sense, is to indicate deference or allegiance, and thus Christ is acknowledged as "Lord" by the Christian. But this, I want to suggest, provides only a very diminished sense of the freight of the title "Lord" in the Apostles' Creed. For just as "Christ" is the Greek stand-in for the Hebrew "Messiah" (anointed one), so LORD, or *Kurios* in the Greek, is stand-in for another Hebrew name for God. But which one? Here the story becomes interesting.

The Hebrew Scriptures that comprise what Christians call the Old Testament were not translated into Greek by Christians but by Jews in the two or three centuries before the birth of Christ. After the conquests of Alexander the Great in the fourth century BCE, Greek became the *lingua franca* of the lands taken as territories stretching right across North Africa and east as far as Persia and Afghanistan. Greek remained the language of the eastern empire after the Romans supplanted the Greeks as rulers, which is the reason the Gospels were written in Greek, not Latin or Hebrew. Hebrew was in fact a dead language by this time, reanimated only in the twentieth century, and most Jews in Palestine and the Levant spoke Aramaic. But the considerable Jewish population of the diaspora—and many in Palestine—spoke or read Greek. Greek was Saint Paul's mother tongue. The Torah in Greek, known as the Septuagint, was most likely translated for the benefit of Alexandria's Greek-speaking Jewish community, the largest Jewish community outside Palestine.

One word defied translation, and that was the Name of the LORD (YHWH). It could not be translated into Greek because, as a proper name (like Fritz or Fiona), it could not be translated at all. This is the Holy Name of God, the four letters called the Tetragrammaton, which we sometimes vocalized as Yahweh. For some centuries before the birth of Christ and down to today pious Jews have not pronounced this Name. Instead in reading aloud when the reader comes to YHWH he or she says "Adonai" that is, the Hebrew for LORD.

In the Hebrew text of Hosea, our first reading for this sermon, we will not read:

> Come, let us return to the LORD;
> for it is he who has torn, and he will heal us;

but

> Come, let us return to the YHWH;
> for it is he who has torn, and he will heal us . . .
> It is YHWH who will come to us like the showers,
> like the spring rains that water the earth (Hos. 1:1a, 3b).

While most English translations hint at the Name lying in the Hebrew original by writing "LORD" in capitals, some English Bible translations, more accurately if less poetically, keep the Hebrew, YHWH, in their text. So did many, probably most, copies of the Septuagint. In these the Greek-speaking Jew read that it is YHWH who creates, YHWH who will redeem his people. Our help is in the Name of YHWH who made heaven and earth. So while the text said YHWH, in praying aloud or reciting the Psalms this same Jewish person would say "our help is in the Name of the LORD." This is to say that "LORD", the Greek word *Kurios*, is already for Greek-speaking Jews and the first Jewish Christians a saturated title . . . . It is carrying the weight of the Holy Name of God.

No place is this more so than in our second reading, from Paul's Letter to the Philippians. This is a very early piece of Christian testimony indeed, earlier than any of the Gospels, and Paul is writing to a group of Jews who had become followers of Jesus. At a certain point the letter incorporates a hymn. It may be that Saint Paul wrote this hymn, but it seems more likely that he was a quoting a praise song already known to his Philippian audience.[4]

> Though he was in the form of God,
> did not regard equality with God

4. See Hurtado, *How on Earth Did Jesus Become a God?*

as something to be exploited,
but emptied himself,
taking the form of a slave,
being born in human likeness.
And being found in human form,
he humbled himself
and became obedient to the point of death—
even death on a cross.
Therefore God also highly exalted him
and gave him the name
that is above every name,
so that at the name of Jesus
every knee should bend,
in heaven and on earth and under the earth,
and every tongue should confess
that Jesus Christ is Lord,
to the glory of God the Father (Phil 2:6–11).

This is even more remarkable when we realize that this praise song is quoting the book of Isaiah from a sequence where God is "addressing the nations", (Isa 45:20) that is, all peoples and not just the people Israel:

The LORD speaks
Turn to me and be saved,
       all the ends of the earth!
  For I am God, and there is no other.
 By myself I have sworn,
   from my mouth has gone forth in righteousness
  a word that shall not return:
  "To me every knee shall bow,
  every tongue shall swear" (Isa 5:22–23).

Paul is making a bold identification that he seems nonetheless to assume will be familiar and uncontroversial to his Jewish Christian audience. This Jesus is the LORD, the one before whom

every knee should bow and every tongue confess. This is to identify Jesus with YHWH, the One through whom all is made, our
Creator and Redeemer.

It is for this reason that I suggest this short verse—which
confesses Jesus to be the Christ, the Son and finally, in a crescendo
of naming, the LORD—is the linchpin of the Apostles' Creed, for
it identifies this Jesus who was born of the Virgin Mary, suffered
under Pontius Pilate, crucified, dead and buried, as the very God
who is Creator of this world and its loving Redeemer. On these
short titles the whole of Christian confession rests. If Jesus is not
this LORD then Christian faith, far from being faith in the Creator
and Redeemer, is mere idolatry.

Bibliography

Bauckham, Richard. *The Theology of the Book of Revelation*. Cambridge:
Cambridge University, 1993.

Dunn, James D. G. *Did the First Christians Worship Jesus?* London: SPCK, 2010.

Hurtado, Larry. *How on Earth Did Jesus Become a God?* Grand Rapids:
Eerdmans, 2005.

Soskice, Janet. "Calling God 'Father.'" In *Kindness of God: Metaphor, Gender,
and Religious Language*, 66–83. Oxford: Oxford University: 2007.

Wilken, Robert Louis. *The First Thousand Years: A Global History of Christianity*
New Haven, CT: Yale University, 2012.

4

"Who was conceived by the Holy Ghost, Born of the Virgin Mary"

MATTHEW BULLIMORE

Isaiah 7:10–17
John 1:43–51

In the summer when I was twelve and my brother was eight my family were on holiday in France. We were driving around looking for a petrol station but they all seemed to be closed. Eventually my parents worked out that it was the Feast of the Assumption and everywhere was shut for the holiday. My mother asked my brother if he knew why it was called the Assumption of the Blessed Virgin Mary. He thought for a moment and then with characteristic Yorkshire matter-of-factness asked: "Is it because they *assume* she was a virgin?"

Why do we assume that Mary was a virgin? And what is the virgin birth or, more properly, the virginal conception all about? We assume Mary was a virgin of course because two of the Gospel writers—in dense and complex birth narratives—tell us that it was so. In Matthew's gospel, Mary is "found to be with child from the Holy Spirit" (Matt 1:18). It fulfils the prophecy of Isaiah—which we heard this evening—that a virgin will bear a child called Emmanuel (Isa 7:10–17) (although the New Revised Standard

Version spoils the effect by translating Matthew in term of the Hebrew text of Isaiah, where *almah* means simply a "young woman"). The Greek rendering of the Hebrew Bible, the Septuagint, uses the Greek word *parthenos*: Matthew uses this word, and it means "virgin". For Matthew, the virginal conception from the Holy Spirit fits well with the point he is hoping to convey about God's involvement with this child: that this Jesus is not only a gift from God but actually *is* somehow Emmanuel—God with us. Luke highlights the virginal conception by having Mary interrogate Gabriel. How can she conceive if she is a virgin? The angelic messenger replies that: "The Holy Spirit will come upon you, and the power of the Most High will overshadow you; therefore the child to be born will be holy; he will be called Son of God" (1:35). Here the virgin birth points us to the truth of *who* Jesus is. In him, God is at work through the power of the Spirit.

However, before we go any further, it is worth going back to our "assumption". Because it seems that other New Testament authors don't necessarily make the same assumption about Jesus' conception. In fact, it might seem that they are unaware of this miraculous element of his birth. They might even work *against* that assumption. In John's gospel, Philip doesn't shy away from identifying Jesus to Nathanael as the son of *Joseph* (1:45). However, it being John, we might wonder if it's not a deliberate misidentification. The point is that appearances can be deceptive. Nathanael soon realises that not only can something good come out of Nazareth but, actually, that good thing happens to be the very Son of God and King of Israel. Yet, that being said, John doesn't mention the strange circumstances of Jesus' conception elsewhere.

Neither the author of the Letter to the Hebrews nor the Gospel of Mark feel the need to make anything of it either. Paul also keeps quiet. He begins his Letter to the Romans by introducing himself as set apart for the Gospel—the Gospel concerning God's Son, "who was descended from David according to the flesh and was declared to be Son of God with power according to the spirit of holiness by resurrection from the dead" (1:3-4). Paul seems to presume Jesus' patrilineal descent from David—and that descent is all very fleshly. Jesus' Sonship still has to do with the Spirit but for Paul it is the resurrection and not Jesus' birth that is the lens through which his Sonship is revealed.

Nonetheless, given the witness of Matthew and Luke and the attestation to the virginal conception in the Creeds, it is a doctrine that we cannot easily pass over. It must have some significance given that twelve precious words of the 109 of the Apostles' Creed are used to describe the circumstances of his birth.

Perhaps the best approach might be for us to ask what work the virgin birth does. As the Nicene Creed tried to clarify, and the Chalcedonian Rule later stated, Jesus is fully human and fully divine. Is this what the virgin birth is meant to point us toward? Is his human nature given to him by his mother and his divine nature given to him by God the Father?

We're on rocky ground here—in danger of making Jesus into something of a demigod—rather like some Greek hero who's the fruit of a strange union between a human mother and a naughty god. The incarnation of the Son doesn't work like that. For a start Jesus is conceived by the Holy Spirit; Mary is overshadowed by the Spirit that descends on her. There is more going on here than just an over-keen cosmic dad. Jesus is not some cut and shut job but *fully* human and *fully* divine.

Anyway, there are good reasons for *not* claiming that Jesus' Sonship rests on the virginal conception. As Austin Farrar, that great Anglican divine, wrote in the last century: "The virginal birth is not the substance of the Incarnation; it is the peculiar way in which (we have been told) it pleased God to bring it about. Jesus is not the Son of God *because* he had no human father."[1] Similarly, the last Pope (Benedict XVI) was quite clear in his early introduction to the faith that: "The doctrine of Jesus' divinity would not be affected if Jesus had been the product of a normal marriage."[2] Jesus' Sonship is something eternally true, not the product of an event in time.

1. Farrer, *The Brink of Mystery*, 21, cited in Lincoln, *Born of a Virgin?*, 19.

2. Ratzinger, *Introduction to Christianity*, 208 cited in Lincoln, *Born of a Virgin?*, 18.

However, there are persistent remnants of that half and half approach in the way in which Matthew and Luke have been read. Ancient biology provided some of the assumptions underlying our later Christian reflections. The Greeks believed that it was a mother who gave the child his or her substance and flesh whilst the father contributed that *je ne sais quoi*—the reason or the form or the character to the child. So Mary could give Jesus all that he needed to be human but it would be God who, like a father, injected Jesus' mind or character.[3] This is a particularly difficult assumption for us for whom biological science is quite clear that a human father provides not just half of the genetic material but specifically the *maleness* through the Y chromosome.

Are we saying at this point then that the virgin birth is more of a barrier to belief than an aid to faithful reflection? After all, how could a man born with no father be fully human? Doesn't the doctrine now *detract* from our understanding of who Jesus is as fully human? It is rarely a good apologetic strategy to invoke at this point the *deus ex machina*. To say "it's just a miracle, accept it" would lead us down the path of thinking that the virgin birth was just about mechanics; that this is simply the mechanism of incarnation. It's how God had to do it and that's that. As the doctrine has been pressed into service over the years there have been approaches that have led us in a mechanical direction. Some believe that the pure virginal conception is the reason that Jesus does not inherit from Adam the original sin that bedevils our lives. The virgin birth becomes a way of ensuring that the bad seed of Adam's kin, the sin of concupiscence, of lustful and base desire, is finally stopped in its tracks. (All of this comes with questionable assumptions about the nature of sex but that's a whole other bag of mashings, as we say in Barnsley.) When the Apostles' Creed is used as the basis of the profession of faith in the baptism service, I have several times heard a suppressed giggle or unbelieving snort when we get to the virgin birth. It's not just that it's scientifically problematic, but it's

---

3. This falls within the remit of the heretical position known as Apollinarianism. See Sweet, "Docetism", 24–31.

almost too miraculous, too mythic, too prudish even. So should we forget it? Or does it still do some important work?

To invoke ideas of a sudden miraculous mechanism or the genetic transmission of sin serves to focus us too much on the virginal conception in isolation—it focuses on the event rather than its place within the whole of Christ's life. It forgets the work that the doctrine performs as a part of that whole. So, despite all that's just been said, I don't think we want to move away from the fact that virgin birth—and its place in the Creed—does refer us back to Jesus' identity as the Son of the Father. Nor should we neglect the role of the Spirit. There is something suggestive about the virginal conception that chimes with Jesus' own self-understanding that he was the Son of his Father in heaven. *Who* he was, his identity, was primarily rooted in his relationship to the God whom he called Father. Fully human as he was, it was not human familial relationships that defined him. Rather, it was who he was as Son of the Father that reveals to us—in and through his humanity—who he was. In his human life of obedience and loving response to the Father's will here amongst us, we see the life of the eternal Son transposed into history. The character of the Son is unchanged. The Son is given to us by the Father in the Spirit and—in some measure—the virgin birth *fits* with that truth. As Farrar said, this is how it "pleased" God to bring about Jesus' birth. It has a certain aesthetic aptness.

We're edging now towards the Trinitarian structure of the Creed as a whole. Perhaps in the end it is to that which the virginal conception points us. Perhaps that is the work it is meant to do. When a creed is working, it helps us to read Scripture well. The Creed begins with creation and directs our attention to the Scriptures where the Father wills to create through the Word as the Spirit hovers over the waters. It is an act of grace, which flows from the work of the triune God. The Creed then moves to the incarnation. We remember that the Father gives us the Son as the Spirit hovers over the waters of Mary's womb and as she assents to the Father's will. Jesus is conceived as an act of Triune grace. (As an aside, it is worth noting that Mary's role is anything but passive.

She is not just the vehicle of incarnation, nor just the source of his flesh. Her character, her faithfulness, her own *Christ-likeness*, is fundamental in the story.) And then the Creed takes us on to the work of new creation that the Son's whole life builds towards. He dies to sin and death. As the Spirit waits in the dark tomb, it is the Father's desire that Jesus is raised. The work of new creation is finally begun. The Creed spells out the repercussions. The new Spirit-led community of the church is called into being—a community of saints that transgresses the limits of death. The Creed reminds us that in this new creation sins are forgiven and the dead are raised.

There is then about the virgin birth a continuing sense of *fit*, of something *behovely* as Mother Julian would say.[4] It is all about grace. It is expressive of God's excessive and transformative grace.[5] The truth of the incarnation is at the heart of a dizzying whirlwind of grace, restoration, recreation, newness and salvation that begins when the Spirit befriends Mary's womb. As we recite the Creed, then, our imaginations can't help but be fired up. As we affirm belief in the virgin birth we begin to hear resonances with the prophets—like Isaiah for whom the young woman and her son Emmanuel are signs of liberation and restoration. We hear echoes of the stories of the barren mothers Sarah and Hannah who prefigure Mary. We remember the new world of which Mary sings where the humble are exalted and the hungry fed.[6]

There's one other set of resonances with which we shall end, and they circle around one person who has only been mentioned in passing—Joseph. There is something pleasing and fitting about Joseph's own role, and how it acts as a counterpart to the relationship we have with our heavenly Father. Joseph adopts Jesus—the Son—into his family. In doing so, he invites God into his own everyday life. He receives the gift of Jesus, and willingly welcomes him into the midst of his own web of relationships—and allows God gently and humbly to accept his hospitality. That adoption

---

4. See Julian of Norwich, *The Showings*.

5. On the Spirit's role and "excess" see Rogers, *After the Spirit*, 98–134.

6. See Williams, "Born of the Virgin Mary", 23–27.

points us to the adoption that *we* enjoy as the fruit of the incarnation. In baptism we become adopted children of God. The Spirit who rests on Jesus, rests on us. The Spirit transforms and renews our humanity and binds us together, forming us into the likeness of Christ. And so we too are adopted into the life of gift, response and love that is the life of God. Farrar puts it better than I could when he says that in worship: "I stand with the divine Son in face of the divine Father, the mantle of his sonship spread around me, and the love of the Father overflowing from him to me in the grace of the Holy Spirit."[7] In our adoption, our humanity is taken up into the life of God and so our lives now shine with his light. The mystery of the incarnation is that Jesus' divinity was revealed through his humanity and not in spite of it. It means that in him we see our humanity perfected, deified; a sign that our own humanness can be caught up into God's life if we welcome him as Mary and Joseph did.

The truth of the gospel—the truth about who Jesus is and the salvation he has wrought—does not stand or fall on belief in the virginal conception. Yet the virginal conception, which is but one part of a whole complex of associations, echoes, and resonances, has led us to meditate on the whole mystery of salvation. Perhaps it is a scandal that we do well to treasure if it leads us deeper into the heart of God's love for us. I for one am not yet ready to cross my fingers at that point in the Creed.

Bibliography

Farrer, Austin, *The Brink of Mystery*. London: SPCK, 1976.

———. "The Trinity in Whom We Live". In *The Truth Seeking Heart: Austin Farrer and his Writings*, edited by Ann Loades and Robert MacSwain, 148–54. London: Canterbury, 2006.

Julian of Norwich. *The Showings of Julian of Norwich*, edited by Denise N. Baker. Norton Critical Edition. London: W. W. Norton, 2004.

Lincoln, Andrew T. *Born of a Virgin? Reconceiving Jesus in the Bible, Tradition and Theology*. London: SPCK, 2013.

Ratzinger, Joseph. *Introduction to Christianity*. London: Burns and Oates, 1969.

7. Farrer, "The Trinity in Whom We Live", 154.

Rogers, Eugene F., Jr. *After the Spirit: A Constructive Pneumatology from Resources Outside the Modern West*. London: SCM, 2006.

Sweet, John. "Docetism: Is Jesus Christ really human or did he just appear to be so?" In *Heresies and How to Avoid Them: Why it Matters What Christians Believe*, edited by Ben Quash and Michael Ward, 24–31. London: SPCK, 2007.

Williams, Rowan. "Born of the Virgin Mary". In *Open to Judgement: Sermons and Addresses*, 23–27. London: DLT, 1994.

5

"Suffered under Pontius Pilate, Was crucified, dead, and buried"

SIMON GATHERCOLE

Isaiah 53
Romans 5:1–11

A few years ago I taught a course at Cambridge's Institute of Continuing Education, after which one of the students on the course made two remarks in his or her feedback form. This student's comments on my teaching and on the Institute's food were jumbled together, so that in the same sentence I read that there was not sufficient attention to the doctrine of the atonement, and—I quote *verbatim*—"rather too much emphasis on root vegetables". I can't at this late stage do anything for this student's digestion, but I can perhaps compensate for what I felt to be a sharp rebuke about the former problem, through the prism of this article of the Creed.

Before embarking on the issue of atonement *per se*, we should observe two things. The first is the glaring ordinariness of this line of the Creed. These words are in one respect utterly uncontroversial. Any respectable ancient historian could cheerfully assent to the proposition that Jesus "suffered under Pontius Pilate, was crucified, died and was buried". What is distinctively Christian about these statements lies in what they mean from God's point of view.

The second point to note at the outset, then, is the paramount consequence of this statement. This comes to the fore in a statement of Paul:

> Now I should remind you, brothers and sisters, of the good news that I proclaimed to you, which you in turn received, in which also you stand, through which also you are being saved, if you hold firmly to the message that I proclaimed to you—unless you have come to believe in vain. For I handed on to you as of first importance what I in turn had received: that Christ died for our sins in accordance with the scriptures, and that he was buried, and that he was raised on the third day in accordance with the scriptures. Whether, then, it is I or they, this is what we preach, and this is what you believed .... Whether then it was I or they, so we proclaim and so you have come to believe (1 Cor 15:1-4, 11).

Paul states here, then, that his subject matter is the "gospel" (in verse 1), this "gospel" is God's instrument of salvation (verse 2), this message is "of first importance" (verse 3), and the message consists of Christ's death for sins and resurrection understood against a Scriptural background (verses 3-4). Moreover, this is not Paul's private message but the gospel message of the whole apostolic college (verse 11). The vicarious death of Christ is thus at the front and centre of Christianity.

I want for the purposes of this chapter, though, to expound another passage in which we see a portrait of Christ as miraculously dying in our place:

> For while we were still weak, at the right time Christ died for the ungodly. Indeed, rarely will anyone die for a righteous person—though perhaps for a good person someone might actually dare to die. But God proves his love for us in that while we still were sinners Christ died for us (Rom. 5:6-8).

We will explore this passage through three lenses—what it says about God, what it says about us, and its explanation of how he treats us.

1. God

First, what does this passage tell us about God? The central point comes in verse 8: "But God proves his love for us in that while we still were sinners Christ died for us." The *love* of God is what is brought to the fore. Now we may think that this is very standard fare, especially in the Bible. But we need to remember that in the Bible this love is not principally about an emotional feeling on God's part. In Scripture, God says clearly that he reveals his love in his actions—and in particular, in that one supreme action: when Christ suffered under Pontius Pilate, was crucified, died, and was buried.[1] What happened in this death of Jesus Christ is described in different ways in Scripture: it is a sacrifice for sins; it delivers us from the power of death; it is a substitution; it is a death in which we share. What is distinctive in this passage in Paul's Letter to the Romans is the passing comment he makes between the two statements about the death of Christ in verse 7: "Indeed, rarely will anyone die for a righteous person—though perhaps for a good person someone might actually dare to die." In the 1 Corinthians passage earlier, there is a strong emphasis on the Scriptural testimony anticipating the gospel. In Romans 5:7, however, Paul is not referring to a theme in Judaism, where an individual dying in place of another is not really much of a topic of discussion. Rather, Paul is tapping into a Greek tradition, a classical tradition according to which it is heroic for one person to die in the place of another. This is a theme in Plato's *Symposium*, his dialogue set in the famous dinner party at which every guest had to make a speech in praise of the god of love, Eros. One of the guests at the dinner, Phaedrus, maintains that only a lover would die in place of another. And the pre-eminent example of this death in place of another, who is cited not only by Plato here but in a number of other authors as well, is Queen Alcestis.

---

1. See also, for example, 1 John 4.9–10: "God's love was revealed among us in this way: God sent his only Son into the world so that we might live through him. In this is love, not that we loved God but that he loved us and sent his Son to be the atoning sacrifice for our sins."

Alcestis is immortalized in the play named after her, written by the poet Euripides around 438 BC. In the opening speech of the play, the god Apollo announces that he has granted the main male character in the play, Admetus the king of Pherae in Greece, the possibility of escaping imminent death if he finds someone to take his place. Only Admetus's wife, Alcestis, was willing to die for him. Alcestis does this, though, in part because neither of Admetus's parents was willing to do it. At one point, Admetus rather uncharitably hurls insults at his father for not dying for him: the father replies coolly, "you haven't died for me—why should I die for you?" His father even jokes that perhaps Admetus's plan is to go on marrying again and again in order to get wives to die in his place so he can live forever. Eventually, Alcestis does indeed die for her husband, although afterwards she is miraculously rescued from the clutches of death by Heracles.

Alcestis's heroic death for her husband fits in with what Paul says here in verse 7: "Perhaps for a good person someone might actually dare to die." Occasionally someone might give up his or her life for a person who is thought supremely worthy.

But not only is Paul tapping into a classical tradition; he is also turning it upside down, in order to spell out how God's love is demonstrated in the Christ who suffered under Pontius Pilate. How? Well to see that we need to look at what the passage says about *us*.

2. Ourselves

Let's consider how *we* are described in the passage:

> For while we were still weak, at the right time Christ died for the ungoldly. Indeed, rarely will anyone die for a righteous person—though perhaps for a good person someone might actually dare to die. But God proves his love for us in that while we still were sinners Christ died for us (Rom 5:6–8).

Paul uses three epithets: "weak," "ungodly," and "sinners". The first, "without strength," or "weak," refers to our lack of moral courage and our inability to withstand temptation. But the problem goes deeper than that, says Scripture: we are not just weak, but also ungodly; it's not that if only we could muster up the strength, we could fulfil our desire to be good people. It is not that we are heading in the right direction but just stop short of our goal. No, as Paul puts it here, we are ungodly: in other words, we are heading in the opposite direction, and running away from God.[2] We are "ungodly" in our attitude to God our Creator; after all, how often do we focus our attention upon him, even though he has made us and given us every good thing we have? Paul goes on to identify us as "sinners" as far as our attitude to his commands is concerned; after all, how often do we focus our attention on doing his will instead of just seeking our own satisfaction?

Notice here, then, that Paul does not say that we are victims, or that we just engage in the occasional guilty pleasure: no, he defines the whole human race—himself, me, all of us included—as "weak", "ungodly", and "sinners". In short, we are specimens of unlovable repellence.

3. God's love for us

Paul doesn't just focus on this point to make us feel miserable, though he does want us to have a proper evaluation of our situation. His main point here is to highlight the extraordinary extravagance of God's love for us. Here, Paul says that the noble deaths of the classical tradition stop being good parallels to the love of God. True enough, there are not just fictional characters like Alcestis who demonstrate this heroic affection for their loved ones, but real individuals who have died for those they love or who share their ideals of friendship. But God demonstrates his love in that even while we are in that condition that Paul has described, God sent

2. The same sequence comes in Romans 8, where in Paul refers first to the weakness of our fallen nature (8:3) and then shortly afterwards to our hostility to God (8:7).

his son to die for us, to rescue us, to bring about that reconciliation with him. Here it is not God for the godly—which would be like the Alcestis example—but God's son dying for the *ungodly*. As Paul's contemporary, the Roman philosopher Seneca, said, it is a noble thing for another human being to die for another worthy person, but it is a wasted benefit to die for someone unworthy (though it is worth saving their life at lesser cost).[3] If we were to imagine someone we think of as an unworthy creature, and ourselves willingly dying in the place of someone like that, we might begin to approximate what it was for God's son to die on the cross *for us*. It had nothing to do with our loveliness, and it was not simply a natural thing to happen. Far from being a predictable historical event, Jesus' suffering and crucifixion under Pontius Pilate is every bit as extraordinary as the creation or the resurrection. The references to Jesus' death in the New Testament are not obituaries but miracle accounts.

In case the objection has arisen in anyone's mind, this is not the heartless dispatch by God of his son, inflicting pain on a third party in order to rescue human beings. Rather, this is God himself coming to save us: "the Son of God, who loved me and gave himself for me," as Paul puts it elsewhere (Gal 2:20). This is the pains to which God went, in order to redeem us. God himself—in the person of the Son—was bearing the death sentence which our guilt had incurred.

When Richard I, Richard the Lionheart, was on his way back from a Crusade, bad weather forced his ship to land in Corfu. Richard and his entourage managed, by disguising themselves as Knights Templar, to reach the European mainland, and so one might have thought all was well. But he was recognised—the story goes, that it was either by his expensive ring, or his insistence on eating roast chicken. The emperor required a ransom of 150,000 marks: to give a sense of how much this was, it amounted to two to

---

3. Seneca, *De Beneficiis* 1.10.5: "A worthy person I would defend even at the cost of my blood and share in his peril; as for an unworthy person, if I can save him from robbers by raising a cry, I would not hold back from speech to save the man."

three times the annual revenue of England. Given what we know about Richard, we might be surprised that our forefathers bothered, but remarkably enough, about a year later the ransom was paid.

For Paul, in this great Epistle to the Romans, God has paid an astronomical ransom for us. Despite the way we have responded—or not responded—to him as our Creator, he has pursued us, and planned to bless us and bring us back to friendship with him. In the words of the hymn, *Praise, my soul, the King of Heaven*, we can be "ransomed, healed, restored, forgiven"—all as a result of God's love for us.

Conclusion

In conclusion, then, we hear in this passage that we are worse than we imagined. God's love does not mean that he looks at us through rose-tinted spectacles, that he overlooks our flaws and—like an indulgent grandparent—only sees our endearing qualities. Rather, God speaks the truth to us about what we really are. Morally bankrupt, in need of a bail-out on a grand scale, a king's ransom. But we don't just hear in this passage that we are worse than we imagined. We also hear that we are more loved than we could ever hope. Not loved in proportion to our loveliness, but the recipients of the greatest divine love that has ever been displayed: in the death of that Jesus Christ, who suffered under Pontius Pilate, crucified, died and was buried—but who now calls us to follow him.

Bibliography

Seneca. *Moral Essays, Volume III. De Beneficiis.* Translated by John W. Basore. Loeb Classical Library. London: Harvard/Heinemann, 1935.

6

"He descended into hell; The third day he rose again from the dead"

ANNA WILLIAMS

Exodus 3
John 12:27–36

*"I will be with you; and this shall be the sign for you that it is
I who have sent you: when you have brought the people out of
Egypt, you shall worship God on this mountain"
(Exod 3:12).*

The portion of Exodus we heard this evening is one of the most famous of all passages of the Old Testament: Moses notices a bush burning in the middle of nowhere, sees that the flames do not consume it, and then hears a voice calling out to him. The burning bush is one of the most dramatic of the biblical theophanies, that is, manifestations of the immaterial and invisible God in the visible and created world. To the atheist, it is yet another legend, a report of something that never happened, a hallucination of someone who does not exist. The Christian might be less inclined to dismiss it so quickly, but might still view it, at best, as one of the stories of things that *used* to happen, and even then, only to extraordinary people like Moses.

The Bible nudges us beyond such modesty, however, because the narrative does not stop where most of us remember the end of the story, with the voice from the bush uttering the mysterious words, "I am who am" (Exod 3:14). The story continues with the voice saying what is not just for Moses' ears, but for the hearing of all the Israelites: "I will be with you." The bush is to be a sign, not of the extraordinary experience of a single person, but of a promise to a whole people, a sign indicating that Moses will lead the children of Israel out of the slavery they endured for centuries in Egypt. The bush is also a marker for the future: the spot where it burns locates the place where the community will eventually worship. The bush has burned, not as a miracle to wonder at for its own sake, but as a sign indicating that the road out of slavery culminates in the intimacy that is the worship of the living God.

My song shall be always of the loving-kindness of the Lord: with my mouth will I ever be shewing thy truth from one generation to another (Ps 89:1).[1]

The words Moses hears from the bush announce not just a message to particular people in their particular circumstances, but the great pattern of the Bible, in a real sense, its one and only story: it is not we who seek God, but God who beckons, calls and leads us towards true joy, a joy so perfect that it is never-ending, that everlasting life which we taste now in worship and in prayer. The promised land lies both ahead of us and in the present moment. It is this pattern which Our Lord Jesus Christ also signals in the intimate prayer recorded in the words from the Gospel of John, which we heard in the second reading: Jesus' first, very human impulse, is to be spared the horror of the crucifixion, "Father, save me from this hour" (John 12:27). He hears his Father's voice and recollects his purpose, "when I am lifted up from the earth, I will draw all

---

1. This sermon was preached with a verse from the psalm set for the day used as an antiphon. A member of the choir stood in the antechapel, beyond the rood screen, and chanted the verse at the points indicated in the text in boldface. I would like to thank the Senior Organ Scholar, Robert Dixon, for his help on this point.

people to myself" (John 12:32). The purpose of the crucifixion is reconciliation, the union of God and humanity made possible by the erasure of the hostility of sin. The pattern is the same as that announced from the burning bush: of the divine mission to the downtrodden, leading them to intimacy with the living God, love's labour of carrying the forlorn beyond hope, to joy.

My song shall be always of the loving-kindness of the Lord: with my mouth will I ever be shewing thy truth from one generation to another.

It is no accident that this pattern should also be the pattern of the creeds, for they tell no more than the story of the Bible in compressed form. In the Apostles' Creed, we begin by affirming belief in the Maker of heaven and earth whose acts are recounted in Genesis. That means we acknowledge our origin in a source greater than ourselves, a source which had no need for us, yet still created us. We are embarrassingly unnecessary, a superfluity, or perhaps better, a luxury, whose sheer existence is only explicable as the fruit of divine love. The central section of the Creed tells the crux of the story, that which follows from this inexplicable creation: the birth, death, and resurrection of the one who in himself unites divinity and humanity, who is both the consummate sign and the consummate medium of humankind's union with God. We acknowledge these central beliefs when we say Jesus Christ was conceived by the Holy Ghost and born of the Virgin Mary, acknowledging him as the one who was sent from the Trinity's heart to become one of us and be one with us, truly human and truly divine, for our good and the good of all the church.

My song shall be always of the loving-kindness of the Lord: with my mouth will I ever be shewing thy truth from one generation to another.

It is humanity's lot, after the fall, that death should follow birth, and at one level, the crucifixion can be understood as no more than the working out of the strict logic demanded once one has asserted that the Saviour is born. We may tend to block out this fact at christenings and Christmas, but there it is: every little bundle of joy, gazed at adoringly by mother and father, is from the moment of its birth under sentence of death; just so, the babe in the manger at Bethlehem, if he is human, must die. That logic, however, is only the pattern that comes into the world at the fall, when human rejection of God meets its logical end, estrangement from the source of life. Like all human creations, that pattern proves temporary. The original divine logic of creation is restated in the coming of the Incarnate Word: the one who was crucified, died and was buried, descended into hell, not to remain forever among the shades, but to bring out those who languished there, to lead them out into the presence of the living God.

This clause of the Creed, "he descended into hell," is one which has little direct biblical support. The Gospels do not tell us what happened between the Friday of the crucifixion and the morning of the following Sunday, when Jesus' tomb was found empty. That is not to say the Creed's claim is *un*biblical. Far from it. As the ancient church understood it, the patriarchs and prophets who were the forerunners of Christ and whose story is told in the Old Testament could not languish forever in a place of dimness far from the light of the living God who spoke to them and whose words they announced for Israel to hear. The logic of the story suggests that even before the discovery of the empty tomb on Easter Day, the tireless divine love must already have been at work, in the proclamation of salvation we now read in the writings of the Old Testament: Christ's first act of saving resurrection is, on the account of the Apostles' Creed, to lead the patriarchs and prophets who speak in its pages to their true home in the everlasting light of the divine presence.

My song shall be always of the loving-kindness of the Lord: with my mouth will I ever be shewing thy truth from one generation to another.

The Apostles' Creed therefore presents Christ as working life (which presupposes he himself lives) even before Easter Day, before the women find the stone rolled away. What we call "the resurrection" is not the event of rising from the grave itself (about this, both the Gospels and the Creeds are silent), but the fact that the living God, the giver of life to all who live and ever have lived, does not abandon his beloved creatures to death. Jesus lives, that he might give life. That death should not have the last word is, from one perspective, a disruption of the logic of life as we know it, the life where death inevitably follows upon birth. From another perspective, however, the resurrection is the restatement of a more fundamental logic, the logic announced at the beginning of the Creed: "I believe in God the Father Almighty, the Maker of heaven and earth". The Maker of all did not create that his beloved creatures might ultimately perish.

One kind of conventional wisdom would of course dispute that the resurrection would in any sense be logical. The resurrection is supposed to be one of the least believable parts of Christian belief ("a fairy story," as I've heard Cambridge academics describe it). Sensible folk know that people do not rise from the dead, and anyway, science tells us it cannot happen.

Really? In the first place, it is not the job of scientists to tell us what has or has not happened in the past. If it is anyone's job, it is that of historians, and they can only tell us what sort of evidence there is for the occurrence of particular events, and render their judgement as to how reliable one might take this evidence to be (which is not quite the same thing as determining whether this or that actually happened). Natural scientists seek to explain natural phenomena. A scientist might say that some phenomenon cannot be explained by the knowledge of the natural world we currently have, but that is not at all the same as saying a particular event could not have taken place. The world the scientist seeks to explain is moreover a vast bundle of mysteries, which far exceeds the capacity of modern science to explain. To take one very mundane example: there is no accepted scientific explanation of how cats purr. This most ordinary phenomenon (kitty gets stroked, kitty purrs) defeats the explanatory powers of zoologists and veterinarians. How do cats do it? It seems only cats know, and they are not telling. Yet cats surely do purr. The fact that something cannot be explained by science does not mean it does not, or did not, happen.

To acknowledge the gaps in our knowledge—or mysteries— is not to claim any kind of proof of extraordinary events, nor does it mean we are bound to believe any tall tale someone might tell us. But investigation into the occurrence of events is, to repeat, the province of the historian rather than the scientist. So can historians prove or disprove the resurrection? It is generally difficult to prove something did not happen. At most, one can say that there is no evidence that it happened. In the case of the resurrection, however, the historical record offers one large phenomenon which is very difficult to account for, but for some utterly extraordinary factor, and that is the sheer existence of the Christian church.

We are so used to thinking of the church as ancient (and perhaps mouldy) that we risk forgetting its very existence is just about a miracle, at least a mystery historians are at a loss to explain. How could a movement started by a lone peasant, whose followers were other peasants, people who had no power in a highly structured regime jealous of its own authority, how could such a movement have endured beyond the gruesome death of its penniless founder? How could that movement spread, literally like wildfire, across the Mediterranean world, with its bazaar of religious and philosophical options clamouring for the hearts and minds of its diverse peoples? How could an uneducated Jewish labourer's teachings have been so compelling that, even in periods of vicious persecution, people believed they were the way of life? As scientists cannot account for the purring of cats, so historians cannot really account for the rise of the Christian church and its endurance through the centuries. There just was not anything about this community that suggested durability beyond the death of its insignificant founder—nothing, except perhaps the community's belief that its founder was still with them.

My song shall be always of the loving-kindness of the Lord: with my mouth will I ever be shewing thy truth from one generation to another.

The existence of the church after the death of Jesus of Nazareth does not prove that the resurrection took place, but the resurrection provides an explanation for the existence of the church—one of the few explanations of a phenomenon that is otherwise very hard to account for. Something occurred after Good Friday that

43

set Jesus' followers aflame, which caused them to believe what the Gospels portray them as doggedly disinclined to believe up until Easter: that Jesus was with them still and would be united to them forever. To put the matter this way is to point to the way in which the resurrection is not a lone item of belief, a fantastic idea assertable only by super-athletes of credulity, leaping over high walls of plausibility with a single bound. The Creeds assert the resurrection in the middle of the narrative, as something inseparably connected to a broader web of assertions. That is why we affirm, after we state our belief in the resurrection, "I believe in the holy Catholic church and the communion of saints". The resurrection explains the existence of the church, just as the source of creation in the divine desire that creatures exist explains the resurrection.

The assertion of the resurrection nestles, then, in the midst of a host of statements, without which it makes little sense. We believe in the origin of all creation in God's ardent desire for creatures who can respond to the divine love; we believe that desire was so strong the Word took our life and form, and lived among us, to be born and to die; and we believe that the Trinity's burning desire for communion with the creature prevailed over our rejection of the good, calling us out of the barren wilderness of alienation from God, whose darkest corner was called Golgotha. And we believe that God's original desire was too powerful to thwarted; that divine love could not end in everlasting estrangement or death; that the Giver of Life who created all things can, did, and does create life anew, calling us to the everlasting worship of the saints of heaven.

You and I stand on holy ground: the Father, the Son and the Spirit call to us here, as surely as they called Moses from the burning bush, as surely as they spoke to the people who heard Jesus say "when I am lifted up, I will draw all people to myself" (John 12:32). We are drawn and called for a purpose: we raise our gaze to the cross that we might worship the living God, the resurrected Lord who is the Giver of life everlasting. And that everlasting life begins here and now when we praise the blessed Trinity and affirm that this praise will continue in the mouths of creatures through the centuries of centuries, world without end.

My song shall be always of the loving-kindness of the Lord: with my mouth will I ever be shewing thy truth from one generation to another.

For I have said, Mercy shall be set up for ever: thy truth shall thou stablish in the heavens.

7

"He ascended into heaven, And sitteth on the right hand of God the Father Almighty; from thence he shall come to judge the quick and the dead"

ANDREW DAVISON

Daniel 7:9–14

Acts 1:1–11

"As they were watching, he was lifted up" (Acts 1:9)

Jesus *ascended* into heaven: he went up. This is a sermon about ascension: not only about *the* Ascension, but about ascension, about going up. I want to explore the theology offered to us by the word *up*. Jesus did not close the forty days after his resurrection with a descent. He did not take his exit in a sideways direction. He went neither down nor sideways: he went up. I want to ask the very simple question, what does "up" mean?

If we step back and think about it, we see that "upwards" ideas permeate our ways of speaking. Upwardness is full of meaning. In 1980, George Lakoff and Mark Johnson published a wonderful book called *Metaphors We Live By*. Lakoff is professor of linguistics at Berkeley, and Johnson a philosopher at the University of Oregon. Their argument is really quite simple: metaphors aren't some special, expressive backwater of language. They are not the reserve of poets and other artistic types. Metaphors are fundamental to the way we use language. They make up the warp and weft of speech. Notice that I have just spoken of language having a "backwater," of the "reserve of poets," and of the "warp and weft of language". These are all metaphors. It is impossible to speak and not use metaphors.

Lakoff and Johnson argued that metaphors underlie the way we speak and think, and I am sure they're right. We express our sense of the world's structure through metaphors, with smaller ones clustering round the bigger ones. And these large-scale metaphors, it turns out, are usually spatial ones: up–down, in–out, deep–shallow, and so on. They are based in our experience of the physical world, and are fairly universal.

Now, it's convenient for our purpose, in thinking about the Ascension, that the principal example that Lakoff and Johnson explore is of "upwards" metaphors. Here is what they say: the language of "up" is associated with happiness, consciousness, and being in control, with quantity, status, virtue, and approval. You'll see why my mind went back to this particular book when wanted to think about what the "up" of the Ascension might mean. Here are some examples of things we say in terms of "up."[1] 'I'm feeling uplifted today' and 'he's feeling down'—that is to say, happy is up. 'Wake up!', 'She rises early', and 'I dropped off to sleep'—conscious is up. 'I have control over it', 'I'm on top of the situation', and 'he fell under my power'—having control is up. 'The share price rose' and 'turn the heat down'—more is up. 'A lofty position', 'she's at the peak of her career', and 'he's climbing the ladder'—status is up. 'High-minded', 'upstanding', 'underhanded', 'a low trick', and 'beneath me'—virtue is up.

Just to show that this isn't simply an analysis of contemporary English, I can add another association to the list from the Old Testament: triumph and confidence are "up". In the Psalms, "lift not up your horn on high" (75:5), and in 1 Samuel, "my horn is

---

1. Many of these examples come from *Metaphors We Live By*.

exalted in my God" (2:1). The church fathers make a link between dignity and "up". Gregory of Nyssa thought that the human form is intrinsically more noble than the body of a pig, because we can lift our heads and see the stars, and the swine cannot. If that reminds us of "I may be in the gutter but at least I am looking at the stars," then it may be the first time that a sermon has seen a conjunction between Oscar Wilde and Saint Gregory of Nyssa's tract *On Virginity*.[2]

What's obvious about all these associations, all these ways of thinking in terms of *up*, is how positive they are. "Up" is associated with happiness, consciousness, control, quantity, status, virtue. Whatever else we could make of that, it underlines that the Ascension concludes the Easter story with a happy ending. That is important to remember. It's ultimately "*up* beat".

There is a tendency in some contemporary Christianity to wallow in the sorrow of the Passion and what gets called "brokenness". It can even be the touchstone of a new orthodoxy. Now, of course, Jesus experienced human suffering to the very end, to the final extreme, but at the resolution he conquered death and sin and evil. We could put it like this: Jesus embraces human tragedy, but his story is not, in the end, a tragedy. It doesn't end in bafflement, compromise, rupture, doom, a stage full of bodies, or any of the other things that students of literature might tell us that tragedy involves. A "Lakoff and Johnson" analysis of "up" language helps us see how much, after the utter darkness and defeat of the Passion, the Ascension strikes a note of resolution and victory. The Ascension underlines the message of the resurrection. The message of Christianity is one of consolation: for all that might arouse urbane, middle class distaste, Christ has won the victory. We had better reconcile ourselves to that, however it might offend those whose cinematic preference, say, is for foreign-language art-house films with grim conclusions.

Looked at another way, the link between the Ascension and upwardsness is one of comprehension. We do not, after all, talk of summing down, but of summing up. And we talk of gathering up,

2. *On Virginity*, 5.

not of gathering down. Christ, we say, is the head of the church, which is his body—the head being at the top. Tenuous though this may seem, it's not: the Ascension is a summing up. It is Christ's journey back to his Father having united himself to us. Jesus, our risen king, is our representative. He sums us all up, just as all of her people are summed up in the Queen, only even more so. He joins us up, he is our head, the keystone of the arch (at the top, notice), he is the first-born from the dead, summing up all creation in himself. This the Pauline language of recapitulation (Eph 1:10),[3] used to such effect by St Irenaeus of Lyon not long after Paul's own time.

Here then is the heart of the message of the Ascension. Christ, our representative, our champion, our hero, our king, has been through hell, and back, for us. And he has triumphed. That is cause enough for celebration on this Ascension Day. But there is more. Jesus is the one who joins all this, all of us, to God and to each other. By the mystery of the incarnation, we are all summed up in Christ. He has triumphed, and we have triumphed with him. All that *up* means for him, it also means for us. As Bishop Christopher Wordsworth (1807–1885) put it,

> He has raised our human nature
> on the clouds to God's right hand;
> there we sit in heavenly places,
> there with him in glory stand:
> Jesus reigns, adored by angels;
> man with God is on the throne;
> mighty Lord, in thine ascension
> we by faith behold our own.[4]

Bibliography

Johnson, Mark, and George Lakoff. *Metaphors We Live By.* 2d ed. Chicago: University of Chicago, 2003.

3. This theme recurs throughout the Pauline literature (as, for instance, also in Rom 5:12–21) and in the Johannine literature (for instance in John 11:52 and 12:32).
4. From the hymn "See the Conqueror mounts in triumph."

8

"I believe in the Holy Ghost"

CHRISTOPHER COCKSWORTH

Isaiah 37:1–14
Acts 1:1–21

*The hand of the Lord came upon me, and he brought me out by
the spirit of the Lord and set me down in the middle of a valley;
it was full of bones. He led me all round them; there were very
many lying in the valley, and they were very dry. He said to me,
"Mortal, can these bones live?" I answered, "O Lord God, you
know." Then he said to me, "Prophesy to these bones, and say
to them: O dry bones, hear the word of the Lord. Thus says the
Lord God to these bones: I will cause breath to enter you, and
you shall live" (Ezek. 37:1–5).*

Jesus: Dead and Raised

The point about Jesus' death is that it was a death. His breath was
no more. It had been asphyxiated out of him by the slow-hanging
torture of crucifixion. His lifeblood no longer moved around his
body. His heart had stopped. His blood had poured out of the side
of his body where it had been pierced by a spear. His body lay in a
tomb and his life was gone. Jesus was dead.

The point about the resurrection was that it was new life: life out of death. It was not a resuscitation of a life that had not fully and utterly died. It was not the revivification of a body that still had capacities for life in it. It was the recreation of life itself. It was a newly creative act akin to the first creation when God breathed the breath of his own life—his *ru'ach*, his own spirit—into the dust that he had formed into the human shape. Here again inanimate matter was being animated by the presence and power of God. That which had no life was given life.

Ezekiel's ancient prophecy was fulfilled: "I will put breath in you and you shall live, and you shall know that I am the Lord" (Ezek 37:6). The resurrection of the dead was happening. The new creation was coming into being. The one whom another and longer creed calls *the Lord and Giver of life* was on the move.

The Disciples: Brought Back to Life

The effect of the death of Christ on his disciples was immediate and complete. The utterly despairing words of Israel belong to the disciples: "our bones are dried up, and our hope is lost: we are cut off completely" (Ezek 37:11). We can hear these words in their panic as they flee from the scene of death. We can hear them in their silence as some of them return to their villages with "downcast faces" (Luke 24:5). We can hear their fear as others gather behind locked doors "for fear of the Jews" (John 20:19). They had been plunged into dull, aching deadness without colour or joy or hope.

The effect of the resurrection of Jesus Christ was more gradual. A woman full of grief-ridden tears hears her name on the lips of a gardener who spoke with the voice of the one who loved her with the purity of divine love. Disappointed, despondent, depressed, disillusioned followers of a failed Messiah had their minds expanded by a stranger, with words that had the quality of God's life-giving word about them, and had their eyes opened by the familiar actions of the Sabbath blessing and breaking of bread. Thomas, a particularly empirically minded disciple who always seemed to take longer than the rest to get the point, was given evidence tailored to the precise needs of his own personality.

The dead Christ into whom the God had breathed his Spirit of life, the Messiah who was raised from the dead by the powerful working of the Lord and Giver of life, was gently bringing life to his disciples in their deadness, to his followers in their fragility of despair, to those who loved him in the lostness of their grief.

And there they were, back in an upper room in Jerusalem, brought back into a life of prayer, re-formed as a community around the figure of Jesus—men and women, close disciples of Jesus and those in the wider group of followers—waiting . . . waiting for the gift of power from on high that the risen Christ had promised (Luke 24:49; Acts 1:8), waiting for the Lord and Giver of life to break them out of the womb of their community into the life of the world.

And the power came with "a sound like the rush of a violent wind" (Acts 2:2) pressing upon them and like the sight of tongues of fire resting on each of them. "O my people, I will put my spirit within you, and you shall live . . ." (Ezek 37:14). And live they do, and speak they do as they burst onto the streets with such an explosion of life and speech that everyone who hears them, so Luke tells us, is "amazed, astonished and perplexed" (see Acts 2:7, 12) with one question on their minds: "what does this mean?" (Acts 2:12).

Peter is not slow in telling them: "Men of Judea and all who live in Jerusalem, let this be known to you, and listen to what I say" (Acts 2:14): the ancient prophecies have been fulfilled, the breath of God has come and the dead bones are being given life. And this is for all Israel—no, for all people on earth: male and female, young and old, every stratum of society including the slaves. Everyone who calls upon the Lord will be saved by the Spirit of God. Every man, woman and child can be brought to life by the Lord and Giver of life by whom God raised Jesus Christ from the dead.

Today: The Meaning for the Church and World

What does this mean for the church today? It means that as well as being a resurrection people who gather around the risen person of Jesus to hear his word, sing God's praises, and enjoy Christ's presence in fellowship and sacrament, we are also to be Pentecost people who are thrust onto the streets of society with an explosion of such demonstrable life that it causes people to say, in our own time, "what does this mean?"

The story of Acts indicates that there are certain prerequisites if this is to happen. One is prayer: the disciples devoted themselves to prayer, we are told. Another is unity: being together in prayer with common accord (see Acts 1:14). The last century began with an invocation to the Holy Spirit that led to a remarkable Spirit-led experience of a common faith. Elena Guerra, founder of the Oblate Sisters of the Holy Spirit, had written twelve letters to Pope Leo calling the Church to that which Lancelot Andrewes, the Anglican Divine of an earlier century had called "the perpetual inspiration of the Holy Spirit". In response Leo initiated the Pentecost Novena, nine days of prayer for the gift of "power from on high" between Ascension Day and the Feast of Pentecost. Then, on the first day of 1901, standing next to the window dedicated to the Holy Spirit in Saint Peter's Basilica, he sang the great hymn to the Spirit, beloved of Anglicans, "*Veni, Creator Spiritus.*" That afternoon, a few thousand miles—both geographical and ecclesiastical—away a group of people were praying in Bethel Bible College, Kansas and a day of Pentecost-type outpouring of the Spirit happened in that small Protestant College that that led to the great revival of 1906, the birth of Pentecostalism and the new charismatic winds of the Spirit blowing through all the churches. The early years of the century also saw the pnuematological turn to the Third Article of the Creed in systematic theology, the rediscovery of the *epiclesis* in liturgical study,[1] and the birth, of course, of the ecumenical movement, in which we all join with Pope John XXIII in prayer for

---

1. The invocation of the Holy Spirit.

the whole world: "Come, Holy Spirit, in your power and might to renew the face of the earth."

The third prerequisite for the church to be a Pentecost people is that we allow the Holy Spirit, the Lord and Giver of life to speak through us in languages that people of the world will hear and understand: the Parthians, Medes, Elamites and the residents of Mesopotamia and every culture and community of this land and of the whole world. That is a tall order but it is not an impossible one. And I say that not only because, as the angel prophesied over Mary about Elizabeth, "nothing will be impossible with God" (Luke 1:37), but also because there is a common language that is shared by all the languages of the world—and that is *the language of life*. Human beings need the gift of life to exist, the preservation of life to maintain life, the fullness of life to thrive, and the hope of life beyond this life to give this life meaning, purpose and ultimate value.

The Lord and Giver of life has given life to us in Christ—the life that brings dry bones to life by the breath of God. We are called to breathe that breath of God deeply with both lungs of the church and then to speak with one voice of the life that God gives: life for the unborn, life for the dying, life for the damaged and disabled, life for the impoverished and oppressed, life for the grieving, life for those seeking to build a new life after the death of a marriage, life for all Syrians, Iraqis and Afghans, life for North and South Sudanese, East and West Ukrainian, Palestinians and Israelis, life for Muslims and life for Christians, life that is not overcome by hate or hurt, by despair or depression, life that is not defeated by death, life for me, life for you: the life of the Lord and Giver of life.

9

"The holy Catholic Church, The Communion of Saints"

ROBERT MACKLEY

Jeremiah 22:1–9, 13–17
Luke 14:27–33

*"For which of you, desiring to build a tower, does not first sit
down and count the cost, whether he has enough to complete it?"*
(Luke 14:28)

Being the relevant, modern "in wi da kids" cleric that I am, a few
months ago I joined—or more accurately, I made my parish
join—Twitter. And given that it was under my church's name—
@littlestmary for those of you minded to follow such things—I
thought I should sign up to follow all sorts of worthy things (rather
than, you know, Waitrose or something), and one such organisa-
tion was Shelter, the homelessness charity. In getting their tweets,
I've become aware that there is a massive shortage of housing in
this country. We might wonder why that is. We're endlessly being
told that the birth rate in northern Europe is now so low as to make
our populations almost unsustainable, and yet here we are apparently with a huge lack of homes. Why? The answer is that more and

more people are living on their own. If present trends continue, apparently, by 2026 40 percent of households will be single occupancy. And so we need a lot more properties. People, it seems, do not like living together—we like our own space, somewhere to retreat to from the world, and we like this more and more. We find other people, and sharing space with them, hard work. All of which must make saying, as we do in the Apostles' Creed, "I believe in the holy, catholic church, and the communion of saints" an experience even more odd for our generation than for the countless generations before us, who have stood in this and every other church around the world and repeated those self-same lines.

For a start you might think that they're just lies. "I believe in the *holy* church": really? Have you met many Christians? Do they all strike you as holy? And if you believed the torrent of negativity poured out by the media about Christianity, you'd think most of us had been giving Satan a run for his money. But alas, there's enough truth amid the exaggerations for saying "I believe in the holy church" to cause more than the odd eyebrow raise. And when we come to "I believe in the catholic church", well, you might say, "no, I don't; I'm not a Roman Catholic, I'm Church of England, thank you very much." And as for "I believe in the communion of saints", well, who knows what that's all about? Perhaps it means we only give Holy Communion to the really good—or maybe not.

In every generation, of course, these bits of the Creed have needed explaining. Now, being the kind of clever people who can just sing something as hard as Stanford's "Double Magnificat" with a grace that made it sound like the easiest thing in the world, you won't need me to tell you that it isn't the case that these lines of the Creed are mere untruths; for the people of the past weren't quite as dim as we sometimes make them out to be. But for our generation they are an especial challenge, for they speak of a faith that really isn't "single occupancy". For yes, we can all name ghastly Christians, and those of us who call ourselves Christians don't have to look far inside ourselves to find plenty of shade to go with the light. But to say, "I believe in the holy church" is not to make a statement about the holiness of *individual Christians*; it is to make a statement about the *church*. And the church is the body of Christ, the pilgrim company of all the baptised. And to say, "I believe in the *holy* catholic church" is to say we believe in a body that is greater than the sum of its parts; that the church is holy not because Robert Mackley or John Hughes are really amazing spiritual people (though obviously your dear Dean is), but because Jesus Christ is holy, and the church is his body. Holiness is not some great achievement of our own, like high school grades or a stunning CV or résumé. It is a gift from God. And it means that even if priests abuse children, Christians go to war, or the parish treasurer embezzles the collection, the game, as it were, isn't up. The church's holiness comes from God and it is a quality not of individual people—though sometimes certain people miraculously do have that quality—but something that manifests itself when we gather together in worship, a thing greater than the sum of our parts, that we achieve not locked in our own rooms with our own thoughts, but when we share as one in prayer and praise as we are now. The glorious music we heard tonight is a reminder and sign of that, for a choir working properly, as yours so clearly does, has a sound that is not just the sum total of twenty or so people. Holiness is unfashionably corporate, communal and indivisible.

In the same way, to say, "we believe in the catholic church" is not to say we believe in a particular branch of Christianity, based in Rome or Canterbury or wherever. For the Greek word "catholic" simply means "*ka holos*": according to the whole. We believe in a faith that isn't "single occupancy," that isn't something I made up, or was the brainwave of a really clever research group. We share a faith common across time and space, a faith according to the whole—not the part. To be a catholic Christian, then, is something we should all aspire to—to be a Christian who shares in the riches and the glory of the whole faith, not just part, not just our favourite bits but that, to use a phrase beloved of the early church, the faith that has been "believed everywhere, always and by all".[1]

---

1. The phrase is from the *Commonitorium* of St Vincent of Lerins (died AD 445).

But that brings us back to our housing shortage. Sharing a household with others is always a piece of work, but in our day and age it is so much harder. We are not accustomed to having our rough and sharp edges smoothed off by rubbing up against other people, for our identities feel too fragile for that. And to suggest that we would want to be part of a family, a church, which contains people of whom we disapprove, and shares beliefs we find hard or plain off-putting is deeply unfashionable. But the alternative is (as it were) ever-increasing single occupancy, not just 40 percent, but eventually 100 percent. However, if we find others hard to live with and share our life with, whether in a physical house or a spiritual church, then we find loneliness even worse. One of the great unspoken modern tyrannies—and that's not too strong a word to use for it—is loneliness. Painful though it is, a sober review of history and of the human condition tells us that "it is", as the Lord says at the beginning of the book of Genesis, "not good for man to be alone" (2:18).

But it is not easy for us to be together either. Most pop songs are indeed about love, yet more lawyers work on divorce than on love. And we can all agree, maybe, that this is the situation and it ought to be changed, but we can't abstract ourselves from our own culture and times—they bear a powerful imprint on us. However, in saying that we believe in the holy, catholic church, the Creed is not just describing an earthly reality now. It is also describing a heavenly future. For the Creed is not a statement of goods like an invoice or a shopping list, but is a prayer—it ends in Amen, after all. And it is a prayer of hope, a prayer of commitment and dedication to what is to come, not just to pious dreams, but to a reality that God promises us will finally be. The Creed looks beyond now and all its pains and difficulties (although any text with the phrases "suffered under Pontius Pilate, was crucified, dead and buried", is not a text that can easily be accused of mindless optimism). So each time we say the Creed we are re-committing ourselves to that holy and catholic future, where we are neither lonely nor suffocated by our neighbour.

We achieve that with the next line of the Creed: "I believe in the communion of saints". The communion of saints is both a description of now and of what will be. For the saints are you and I, as Saint Paul teaches, and it is all the baptised; all of us are on the way to being saints, however distant that may feel! In heaven everyone is a saint, everyone has that holiness that shines more brightly than the sun; and because they share in our baptism, they are in communion with us. *Communion* is another word for that phrase with which the Book of Common Prayer ends evensong— "The grace of our Lord Jesus Christ, the love of God and the fellowship of the Holy Spirit be with us all evermore." The fellowship of the Holy Spirit: it could just as well be translated "communion of the Holy Spirit". For communion, fellowship, is that life that the Holy Spirit gives to us, that life that is neither loneliness nor suffocation. To believe in the communion of saints is to believe and hope in a life together which, when it works, is so glorious it makes Stanford's "Magnificat for Double Choir" sound like a bad rendition of "Happy Birthday to You". And because those made perfect in the kingdom of heaven have fellowship, have communion with us on earth with all our rough and jagged corners, even now we are not alone. The saints in heaven cheer us on and pray for us—as the Letter to the Hebrews and the book of Revelation make clear—they pray for us that even in our single rooms we may know ourselves to be in a house with many mansions (John 14:2); that even in our frustration with our neighbour, we may also see in him or her something we want to share; and even now as we tweet about our lack of housing, we may lay hold of our communal home in heaven.

10

"The Forgiveness of sins, The Resurrection of the body, And the Life everlasting. Amen."

SAM WELLS

Isa. 40:6–11
Mark 2:1–12

The present doesn't exist. I don't mean that I'm not speaking to you now, that we're not really here, that Cambridge in the entirety of its vast knowledge, culture, activity, and ego is an illusion. I mean that as soon as you try to put your finger on the present tense—bang!—like a horsefly under a slapping hand, it's gone. There's no such thing as the present tense. It's a construction designed to make us feel alive.

As soon as we realise this we become subject to two primal, visceral, and existential terrors. The first terror is this: you can't stop time. It's out of control. It's like Canute trying to stop the incoming tide. It's an ever-rolling stream, and it's going to roll you away just as it's rolled away all its sons and daughters beforehand. When Muhammad Ali says, "I am the greatest of all time," or a World War I memorial reads, "their names shall live for evermore," the pathos is comical or unbearable: have these people no notion of eternity? We are profoundly ephemeral—as permanent as a feather on the wind. The second terror is this: what we've done can't be undone. However much we try to retell the story, airbrush the photographs, fiddle with the timings on the emails, deny, pretend, fabricate, or wriggle, there's no changing what's happened. Our histories are made up of folly, failure, and fecklessness. And we can't alter them.

These two terrors—the panic about the past and the fear of the future—constitute the prison of human existence. There's no such thing as the present tense because it's no more than the overlap between the past and the future. And there's no genuine living in the present tense because our lives are dominated by regret and bitterness and grief about the past and are paralysed by fear and anxiety and terror about the future. The present has become tense without being truly present.

Think about your life. Think about what grieves you. I'm guessing it's what's happened in the past that you can't change, the sequence of events that's led to a kind of prison, has led to you being in some sense in chains. And I'm guessing it's the things you cherish that you dread you can't keep—your youth, your life, the things and the people you love, this very moment we share right now.

And what does the Christian faith proclaim? Two central convictions. One about the past, and one about the future.

The first is about the past. It's the forgiveness of sins. Forgiveness doesn't change the past. But it releases us from the power of the past. Forgiveness doesn't rewrite history: but it prevents our histories asphyxiating us. Fundamentally, forgiveness transforms our past from an enemy to a friend, from a horror show of shame to a storehouse of wisdom. In the absence of forgiveness we are isolated from our past, trying pitifully to bury or deny or forget or destroy the many things that haunt and overshadow and plague and torment us. Forgiveness doesn't change these things: but it does change their relationship to us. No longer do they imprison us or pursue us or surround us or stalk us. Now they accompany us, deepen us, teach us, train us. No longer do we hate them or curse them or resent them or begrudge them. Now we find acceptance, understanding, enrichment, even gratitude for them. That's the work of forgiveness. It's about the transformation of the prison of the past.

This isn't about willpower or determination or self-help. This is the work of Jesus. Jesus walks beside us, and the negative aspects of those past experiences he takes into his body, leaving us with the memories that can strengthen, deepen, and ennoble us. That's the perpetual work of the cross. Jesus takes upon himself the evil that we have done and that has been done to us, facing the unimaginable agony of it all, and thereby gives us back our past as a gift and not a threat. Our chains fall off, our heart is free. Nothing, in the end, is wasted. All is redeemed. Just bask for a moment in the wonder of being released from the prison of the past. It's almost beyond our imaginations. It's the gift of the gospel.

Here's the second conviction. It's about the future, the life everlasting. Everlasting life doesn't take away the unknown element of the future, but it takes away the paroxysm of fear that engulfs the cloud of unknowing. Everlasting life doesn't dismantle the reality of death, the crucible of suffering, the agony of bereavement, but it offers life beyond death, comfort beyond suffering, companionship beyond separation. In the absence of everlasting life, we're terrified of our future, perpetually trying to secure permanence in the face of transitoriness, meaning in the face of waste, distraction in the face of despair. Everlasting life doesn't undermine human endeavour, but it rids it of the last word; evil is real, but it won't have the final say; death is coming, but it doesn't obliterate the power of God; identity is fragile, but in us that resides in God, and will be changed into glory.

This isn't about fantasy. I am not "a thousand winds that blow".[1] Death is certainly not "nothing at all".[2] This is the work of Jesus. By rising from the dead Jesus turns death from a wall into a gate, from an obliteration to a threshold, from an emptying of meaning to a testing of trust. Jesus goes into the refiner's fire and

1. From the poem by Mary Elizabeth Frye, "Do not stand at my grave and weep".

2. From a sermon by Henry Scott-Holland (where this phrase was not advanced without criticism).

refashions for us a new life out of the one from which all sin has been burnt away. Death is turned from the moment of absolute eternal isolation into the entrance to utter everlasting companionship. We call it heaven. We're given back our future as a gift, and not a threat. Everything is possible. Bask for a moment in the gift of everlasting life. Feel it slowly dismantle all your worst fears. Let it set you free. Let it give you indescribable joy.

This is the Christian faith. The newspapers think it's all about women bishops and gay marriage. Of course those things matter. But the heart of it all is forgiveness of sins and the life everlasting. If you have those, nothing can finally hurt you. If you don't have those, nothing can save you.

In between forgiveness and everlasting life, the Apostles' Creed puts the resurrection of the body. Why? Well, in the first place, about Jesus, that's easy. Jesus' resurrection makes possible and embodies the forgiveness of sins. Jesus is betrayed during his passion three times by Peter; Jesus in his resurrection restores Peter three times. The appearance of the embodied Jesus, inhabiting the same body as was crucified two days before, proves that the worst we can do is still not enough to determine the ultimate course of history, and not enough to alter God's decision to be with us in Christ. Meanwhile Jesus' resurrection proclaims the life everlasting. Death is no longer an insuperable barrier. In Jesus we've all been given a glimpse of restoration beyond obliteration. The body's not a prison to be escaped or a ladder to be kicked away; it's the shape of our future in Christ. Thus resurrection turns the past from dungeon into heritage and the future from fate into destiny.

But the resurrection of the body is about us as well as about Jesus. Remember where I started. There's no such thing as the present tense. Well there isn't, if there's no forgiveness and no life everlasting. But wait. If there *is* forgiveness—if the past is a gift, and if there *is* everlasting life—if the future's our friend, then for the first time we really can live—we really can breathe, we really can relax, we really can exist. We really are a new creation. Every detail of our lives is precious and wonderful and beautiful and meaningful, rather than passing and pitiful and feeble and futile. This is nothing less than a new birth. This is our present—God's present to us; God's presence with us. This is resurrection.

28379989R00047

Printed in Poland
by Amazon Fulfillment
Poland Sp. z o.o., Wrocław